Heinemann is an imprint of Pearson Education Limited,
a company incorporated in England and Wales, having
its registered office at Edinburgh Gate, Harlow, Essex, CM20 2JE.
Registered company number: 872828

Heinemann is a registered trademark of Pearson Education Limited

First published in 1949
First published in the *Hereford Plays* series by Heinemann Educational 1968
First published in the *Heinemann Plays* series 1994

31

A catalogue record for this book is available from the British Library on request.
ISBN: 978 0 435233 07 5

Cover photo: Getty

Typeset by TechType, Abingdon, Oxon

Printed in China (CTPS/31)

CONTENTS

Preface   v
Introduction   vii
List of Characters   xvii

Death of a Salesman
    Act One   1
    Act Two   50
    Requiem   106

Questions and Explorations
1 Keeping Track: Act One   109
                  Act Two   110
                  Requiem   111
2 Explorations: A Characters   111
                  B Themes   115
                  C Criticism   116

PREFACE

In this edition of *Death of a Salesman,* you will find notes, questions and activities to help in studying the play in class, particularly at GCSE level.

The introduction provides background information on the author and his other works, the historical basis to the play and the circumstances and impact of its first production.

The activities at the end of the book range from straight-forward *Keeping Track* questions which can be tackled at the end of each act to focus close attention on what is happening in the play, through more detailed work on characters and themes in *Explorations*, to more advanced discussion questions under *Criticism*.

If you are already using the Hereford edition of *Death of a Salesman*, you will find that the page numbering in the actual playscript is the same, allowing the two editions to be easily used side by side.

INTRODUCTION

Arthur Miller

Arthur Miller was born in New York in 1915. His Austrian father had come to America, the land of opportunity, where he had made a prosperous living as a clothing manufacturer. When the Stock Market crashed in 1929 and recession followed, the family business was ruined and there was no money to send Miller to university. He paid for his own studies by taking a variety of jobs and while at the University of Michigan he studied Economics, History and, rather later, journalism and play-writing.

His most successful plays were; *All My Sons* (1947), *Death of a Salesman* (1949), *The Crucible* (1953) and *A View from the Bridge* (1955). *All My Sons* and *Death of a Salesman* have common themes: an individual in business who is trying to make his way in a society which has become strange and hostile. Values which once seemed important in society now carry little weight and the protagonists in both plays smash themselves to pieces as a result of their inability to adjust to these changing and declining living standards.

Death of a Salesman

The chance to achieve great things which drew Miller's father to America inspired a whole generation to believe that with hard work and belief in themselves they could achieve their ambitions of wealth and personal status. This ideal – the Great American Dream – expressed the longings of people who wanted to break new ground in a developing country, to amass money and enjoy a comfortable lifestyle, to work for themselves and not be at an employer's beck and call.

This capitalist system of free enterprise and big business undoubtedly had its rewards. It was not without its problems, too, and in Willy Loman we see a man who has fallen foul of this system. He is 'worked out' and in the ruthless world of business there is no room for sentiment: if he can't do the work then he is no good to the firm and he must go.

Although Willy is painfully a victim of this system, his loyalties demand that he continues to serve it and he is bewildered at his lack of success. He has to hide behind a smoke screen of lies and pretence to disguise the fact to others and himself that he has failed. The ploy with Howard, when he insists he too will buy one of the new fangled tape recorders, is a sad reminder of his failure. He has no money for tape recorders – indeed he cannot even pay the bills. Salesmen were at the cutting edge of the American Dream – the original self-made men who sold not their goods, but their personalities.

Equally powerful in this concept is the romantic vision of the 'great outdoors', rural living close to nature. Here a different sort of dream can be realised, but one which strikes a wistful note in Biff: 'We don't belong in this nuthouse of a city. We should be mixing cement on some open plain ...'

The pioneer combines these two visions: Ben is the focus of this stereotype. He is determined to be rich and leaves the city for unexplored countries and 'the jungle' where he is dealing in diamonds and establishing his own very profitable business.

Willy, at 60, looks at what he has achieved and sees very little. Lacking Ben's ruthlessness, he failed to grasp the opportunity Ben offered him. He is too rooted in the past to see that the popularity he enjoyed in his early days of selling has now dwindled almost to nothing. It is one of the saddest moments of the play when Miller makes us aware that no one attended Willy's funeral. Willy was so sure that it would be a positive experience, proving to Biff how well-liked he was. Linda's desperate cry 'Why didn't anyone come?' is equally deeply felt by the audience. Although he was deluded by false values, Willy has served the system loyally and now that he is in his declining years he is rejected by it in the coldest way. It is a poignant moment in the play when we see him planting seeds in his back yard in a last futile effort to leave something of value behind which will outlive him.

Miller and capitalism

It is obvious that *Death of a Salesman* is a powerful attack on the American system, with its ruthless, aggressive business tactics and its insistence on money and social status as indicators of worth.

Miller himself was no stranger to conflict with the American way of life. Since 1938, an organisation called the House Un-American Activities Committee had been in existence in America. This had the power to investigate any person who apparently threatened the safety of the state. Under the chairmanship of Senator Joseph McCarthy, this committee became almost paranoid in its searching out of communist sympathisers in the 1940s and 1950s. Suspects were brought before the committee to answer charges that they were communist sympathisers. Miller was summoned before the McCarthy commission in 1956 and accused of communism and a desire to undermine the American way of life. Miller strenuously denied this saying, 'In truth, I had supported these various causes to express my fear of a looming victory of fascism and my alienation from the waste of potential in America while knowing nothing about life under any socialist regime'. However, he was found guilty and his career and personal life were, for a time, much affected by this verdict.

Critics have interpreted *Death of a Salesman* as an attack on the values of which he disapproves, an attempt to bring the capitalist structure into disrepute. Such a reading of the play is too superficial and misses what Miller really wants us to understand. The play is not about capitalism or communism but about a man disillusioned by the passage of time and horrified at the realism that it has robbed him of dreams, ambitions and success. This is why we see Willy at the end of his career, not at the beginning. We can see more plainly how total his failure is in the eyes of the society in which he lives.

The tragic hero

Our dramatic tradition comes from the Greeks and is more directly descended from Shakespeare. He took the idea of tragedy and adapted it to his own ends. Shakespearean tragic heroes fit a pattern: they are of noble birth, they have a fatal character flaw, for example, an ability to fall in love too quickly and too deeply like Romeo in *Romeo and Juliet* and they or those around them must learn from their mistakes. Finally, all Shakespeare's tragic heroes die as a result of this character flaw. These criteria have become established as defining a tragic hero.

Willy Loman does not fit into these criteria in one telling way – he is not of noble birth. In fact, Miller was determined that he should be an ordinary man in order to demonstrate the fate of those anonymous people – perhaps like us – who, in their millions support a system which casts them aside when they need it most. Miller felt 'It matters not at all whether a modern play concerns itself with a grocer or a president, whether the hero falls from a great height or a small one'. What matters is 'the intensity of the human passion to surpass his given bounds' and 'the questions whose answers define humanity and the right way to live'. Shakespeare's heroes were motivated by high passions such as lust, greed and ambition but Miller suggests that these are no more important or admirable than Willy's determination to be well-liked. Like the lives and deaths of Shakespeare's heroes, Willy Loman's life and death poses the question: 'What do men live for?'

Like Shakespeare's tragic heroes Willy is universal in the sense that he embodies hopes, dreams and fears which could be typical of all of us. We all know what it feels like to strive to succeed. We all know how bitter the taste of failure is. We may be reluctant to confess how much material success means to us, we may even be ashamed of it, but it is often an inescapable part of all our daily lives.

Does Willy learn from his mistakes? What about those around him? Willy seems to have learned at the end of the play that Biff loves him and forgives him for his earlier mistake in the affair with the Woman. However, he has misunderstood Biff's cry of frustration and despair and subsequent tears (Act Two) as an expression of love. Linda certainly learns nothing from his death and fails to understand his actions. Happy vows at his graveside that he will continue to try to realise his father's dream – the antithesis of intellectual progress.

Willy dies, as tragic heroes must do, but his death affirms the beliefs to which he has clung and which have destroyed him. He commits suicide in order to secure a substantial insurance payment for Biff because he believes that the only true value of a man's worth is how much he is liked and how much he has. He believes this money will set Biff up in business, opening doors for him and enabling him to persuade people to his way of thinking. It is tragic indeed, that a man's death should make him a sacrifice on the altar of the belief which has failed him.

It is interesting to consider whether or not Willy Loman is a tragic hero because it helps us to explore what the play means for us. However, what matters in the end is not deciding whether the play is a tragedy or whether Willy is a tragic hero but responding to the power of the story and to the vital things the play has to say. As Arthur Miller wrote: 'I set out not to write a tragedy but to show the truth as I saw it.'

Staging of the play

The play shows a series of chronological events which take place during one evening and the next day. At intervals throughout the play we see scenes from Willy's past enacted on the same stage set at the same time. On first consideration this seems more likely to confuse than reveal, but Miller had very strong reasons for staging the play in this way.

It is Miller's belief that the past is not something which is now behind us. Miller asserts that the past is with us all the time, informing and influencing our actions and choices. If we are to understand Willy, we must be aware of the emotional burdens and the formative influences which he carries with him from the past.

The scenes from the past also serve another purpose: to correct the audience's images of events and characters seen through Willy's eyes. It is the distance between Willy's judgements and recollections and the reality with which the 'flashbacks' confront us that helps us to understand Willy as a character and to be aware of the seriousness of his decline.

Miller does not need to use the chronological series of events to create suspense and keep his audience wondering what happens next. It is obvious from the moment Willy steps onto the stage that he is a man close to despair and at the end of his physical and emotional strength. Throughout his flashbacks, Miller reveals how Willy degenerated and why he lost his hope of a successful and popular life.

Characters

WILLY LOMAN

Willy Loman never comes to terms with reality. He lives in his dreams and derives all his pleasures from the past, which he distorts to convince himself that all is well. His role models are the great salesmen of a bygone age who sold their personalities first and their goods second. These heroes are out of place in the modern business world where ruthless aggression gains results.

Pride is central to Willy's character: pride in being (or pretending to be) a successful salesman, pride in his sons (especially Biff) and pride in being independent – he refuses Charley's help when he has lost his job and needs it most.

Although Willy is never able to attain his ideals and his life is a massive self-deception he still retains his hopes. Even as he contemplates suicide, he is hopeful that the insurance money payable on his death will give Biff the start he needs.

BIFF LOMAN

Biff has never realised his potential and remains unsure of himself. Willy has built Biff a structure of self-deceit which has prevented him from seeing clearly his strengths and weaknesses. He has not made his way in the world and seems unable to see the direction in which he wants to go. He admires Willy but has been disillusioned by his affair with the Woman and so lacks motivation in realising his niche in society: his inspiration, derived from Willy, has been tarnished.

He realises too that the family has been built on an edifice of deception and can no longer subscribe to it by pretending to be what he is not. He refuses to live a lie and enter half-heartedly into the world of business. His real interests lie in a rural existence, away from the falsity and corruption of the city but he is too undisciplined to channel his energies in a positive career direction.

HAPPY LOMAN

Happy is as equally committed to the capitalist system as Willy but he cannot admit that. Like Willy, he has failed. Like Willy, he wants success and respect but his weaknesses – most notably for women – deny him these things.

He sees Biff as his road to success and so it is inevitable that his dreams will remain unrealised. Again, like Willy, he has to pretend to be more than he really is – an assistant buyer instead of one of two assistants to the assistant.

He learns nothing about himself, unlike Biff, and he fails to realise the implications of Willy's death for his own ambitions. Biff continues to practise the self-deception which is a common trait of the Loman family and is incapable of understanding that he must face reality if he is ever to make anything of himself.

LINDA LOMAN

Linda is, above all else, loyal to Willy and his hopes and ideas. She suffers as he visibly deteriorates because she knows there is nothing she can do to help him. She has always believed that Willy is the best in all respects and it would be easy to question her judgement. It would be wrong to do so, since it is her unquestioning faith in the need to treat people properly which gives her strength and dignity.

She desires only to be happy with what she has: Ben's proposals frighten her and she is angry with Biff and Happy when they expect the status quo of family life. She has never fully understood Willy or her sons – their desire for freedom away from the city bemuses her. She would like to be free, but from financial worries, and she sees her life in the city, not elsewhere.

BEN LOMAN

Ben is a symbol of the new style of businessman – the entrepreneur, willing to risk everything in a daring venture and ready to thrust ruthlessly aside those who get in his way.

He is free, intellectually and emotionally, in a way which Willy is not and this enables him to become rich because he is completely at liberty to do what he chooses. When he urges Willy to join him, he forgets that Willy has a home, a wife and a family to support.

BERNARD

Ben provides a contrast to Willy just as Bernard does with Biff. He has got to the top of his profession and achieved all the things which Willy wanted for Biff. He does not push his success into the Lomans' faces, however, he remains tactful and sympathetic.

Willy refuses to accept his help, just as he refused to accept his warnings about Biff in earlier years. Bernard, therefore, must stand and watch since he is not allowed to help.

CHARLEY

Charley, too, is sympathetic towards Willy and his family, lending him money when he is desperate and trying to cheer him out of his darkest moods. This is what he has to offer in the play and money will not solve Willy's problems. They go much deeper than this and Charley cannot solve psychological dilemmas. So, like Bernard, he must stand and watch since he cannot help.

HOWARD WAGNER

Howard takes only a small part in the play but is a powerful symbol of the modern businessman. He puts the firm first and when Willy can no longer contribute to it, he sacks him, with no regard for his loyal service or his friendship with his father.

He is insensitive, parading a tape recorder which he knows Willy cannot afford, but he is honest – he does not have a job for Willy and is too much the professional businessman to manufacture one.

Val Randall

List of Characters

WILLY LOMAN
LINDA
BIFF
HAPPY
BERNARD
THE WOMAN
LETTA
CHARLEY
UNCLE BEN
HOWARD WAGNER
JENNY
STANLEY
MISS FORSYTHE
WAITER

The action takes place in Willy Loman's house and yard and in various places he visits in the New York and Boston of today.

DEATH OF A SALESMAN

ACT ONE

A melody is heard, played upon a flute. It is small and fine, telling of grass and trees and the horizon. The curtain rises.

Before us is the Salesman's house. We are aware of towering, angular shapes behind it, surrounding it on all sides. Only the blue light of the sky falls upon the house and forestage; the surrounding area shows an angry glow of orange. As more light appears we see a solid vault of apartment houses around the small, fragile-seeming home. An air of the dream clings to the place, a dream rising out of reality. The kitchen at centre seems actual enough, for there is a kitchen table with three chairs, and a refrigerator. But no other fixtures are seen. At the back of the kitchen there is a draped entrance, which leads to the living-room. To the right of the kitchen, on a level raised two feet, is a bedroom furnished only with a brass bedstead and a straight chair. On a shelf over the bed a silver athletic trophy stands. A window opens on to the apartment house at the side.

Behind the kitchen, on a level raised six and a half feet, is the boys' bedroom, at present barely visible. Two beds are dimly seen, and at the back of the room a dormer window. (This bedroom is above the unseen living-room.) At the left a stairway curves up to it from the kitchen.

The entire setting is wholly or, in some places, partially transparent. The roof-line of the house is one-dimensional; under and over it we see the apartment buildings. Before the house lies an apron, curving beyond the forestage into the orchestra. This forward area serves as the back yard as well as the locale of all WILLY'S *imaginings and of his city scenes. Whenever the action is in the present the actors observe the imaginary wall-lines, entering the house only through its door at the left. But in the scenes of the past these boundaries are broken, and characters enter or leave a room by stepping 'through' a wall on to the forestage.*

From the right, WILLY LOMAN, *the Salesman, enters, carrying two large sample cases. The flute plays on. He hears but is not aware of it. He is past sixty years of age, dressed quietly. Even as he crosses the stage to the doorway of the house, his exhaustion is apparent. He unlocks the door, comes into the kitchen, and thankfully lets his burden down, feeling the soreness of his palms. A word-sigh escapes his lips – it might be* 'Oh, boy, oh, boy.' *He closes the door, then carries his cases out into the living-room, through the draped kitchen doorway.* LINDA, *his wife, has stirred in her bed at the right. She gets out and puts on a robe, listening. Most often jovial, she has developed an iron repression of her exceptions to* WILLY'S *behaviour – she more than loves him, she admires him, as though his mercurial nature, his temper, his massive dreams and little cruelties, served her only as sharp reminders of the turbulent longings within him, longings which she shares but lacks the temperament to utter and follow to their end.*

LINDA   (*hearing* WILLY *outside the bedroom, calls with some trepidation*) Willy!

WILLY   It's all right. I came back.

LINDA   Why? What happened? (*slight pause*) Did something happen, Willy?

WILLY   No, nothing happened.

LINDA   You didn't smash the car, did you?

WILLY   (*with casual irritation*) I said nothing happened. Didn't you hear me?

LINDA   Don't you feel well?

WILLY   I'm tired to the death. (*The flute has faded away. He sits on the bed beside her, a little numb.*) I couldn't make it. I just couldn't make it, Linda.

LINDA   (*very carefully, delicately*) Where were you all day? You look terrible.

WILLY   I got as far as a little above Yonkers. I stopped for a
        cup of coffee. Maybe it was the coffee.

LINDA   What?

WILLY   (*after a pause*) I suddenly couldn't drive any more.
        The car kept going off on to the shoulder, y'know?

LINDA   (*helpfully*) Oh. Maybe it was the steering again. I
        don't think Angelo knows the Studebaker.

WILLY   No, it's me, it's me. Suddenly I realize I'm goin' sixty
        miles an hour and I don't remember the last five
        minutes. I'm – I can't seem to – keep my mind to it.

LINDA   Maybe it's your glasses. You never went for your
        new glasses.

WILLY   No, I see everything. I came back ten miles an hour.
        It took me nearly four hours from Yonkers.

LINDA   (*resigned*) Well, you'll just have to take a rest, Willy;
        you can't continue this way.

WILLY   I just got back from Florida.

LINDA   But you didn't rest your mind. Your mind is over-
        active, and the mind is what counts, dear.

WILLY   I'll start out in the morning. Maybe I'll feel better in
        the morning. (*She is taking off his shoes.*) These
        goddam arch supports are killing me.

LINDA   Take an aspirin. Should I get you an aspirin? It'll
        soothe you.

WILLY   (*with wonder*) I was driving along, you
        understand? And I was fine. I was even observing
        the scenery. You can imagine, me looking at the
        scenery, on the road every week of my life. But
        it's so beautiful up there, Linda, the trees are so
        thick, and the sun is warm. I opened the wind-
        shield and just let the warm air bathe over me.
        And then all of a sudden I'm goin' off the road! I'm
        tellin' ya, I absolutely forgot I was driving. If I'd've
        gone the other way over the white line I might've
        killed somebody. So I went on again – and five
        minutes later I'm dreamin' again, and I nearly – (*He*

presses two fingers against his eyes.) I have such thoughts, I have such strange thoughts.

LINDA Willy, dear. Talk to them again. There's no reason why you can't work in New York.

WILLY They don't need me in New York. I'm the New England man. I'm vital in New England.

LINDA But you're sixty years old. They can't expect you to keep travelling every week.

WILLY I'll have to send a wire to Portland. I'm supposed to see Brown and Morrison tomorrow morning at ten o'clock to show the line. Goddammit, I could sell them! (*He starts putting on his jacket.*)

LINDA (*taking the jacket from him*) Why don't you go down to the place tomorrow and tell Howard you've simply got to work in New York? You're too accommodating, dear.

WILLY If old man Wagner was alive I'd a been in charge of New York now! That man was a prince, he was a masterful man. But that boy of his, that Howard, he don't appreciate. When I went north the first time, the Wagner Company didn't know where New England was!

LINDA Why don't you tell those things to Howard, dear?

WILLY (*encouraged*) I will, I definitely will. Is there any cheese?

LINDA I'll make you a sandwich.

WILLY No, go to sleep. I'll take some milk. I'll be up right away. The boys in?

LINDA They're sleeping. Happy took Biff on a date tonight.

WILLY (*interested*) That so?

LINDA It was so nice to see them shaving together, one behind the other, in the bathroom. And going out together. You notice? The whole house smells of shaving lotion.

WILLY Figure it out. Work a lifetime to pay off a house. You finally own it, and there's nobody to live in it.

LINDA Well, dear, life is a casting off. It's always that way.

WILLY No, no, some people – some people accomplish something. Did Biff say anything after I went this morning?

LINDA You shouldn't have criticized him, Willy, especially after he just got off the train. You mustn't lose your temper with him.

WILLY When the hell did I lose my temper? I simply asked him if he was making any money. Is that a criticism?

LINDA But, dear, how could he make any money?

WILLY (*worried and angered*) There's such an undercurrent in him. He became a moody man. Did he apologize when I left this morning?

LINDA He was crestfallen, Willy. You know how he admires you. I think if he finds himself, then you'll both be happier and not fight any more.

WILLY How can he find himself on a farm? Is that a life? A farmhand? In the beginning, when he was young, I thought, well, a young man, it's good for him to tramp around, take a lot of different jobs. But it's more than ten years now and he has yet to make thirty-five dollars a week!

LINDA He's finding himself, Willy.

WILLY Not finding yourself at the age of thirty-four is a disgrace!

LINDA Shh!

WILLY The trouble is he's lazy, goddammit!

LINDA Willy, please!

WILLY Biff is a lazy bum!

LINDA They're sleeping. Get something to eat. Go on down.

WILLY Why did he come home? I would like to know what brought him home.

LINDA I don't know. I think he's still lost, Willy. I think he's very lost.

WILLY Biff Loman is lost. In the greatest country in the world a young man with such – personal attractiveness, gets lost. And such a hard worker. There's one thing about Biff – he's not lazy.

LINDA Never.

WILLY (*with pity and resolve*) I'll see him in the morning; I'll

have a nice talk with him. I'll get him a job selling.
He could be big in no time. My God! Remember
how they used to follow him around in high school?
When he smiled at one of them their faces lit up.
When he walked down the street ... (*He loses
himself in reminiscences.*)

LINDA (*trying to bring him out of it*) Willy, dear, I got a new
kind of American-type cheese today. It's whipped.

WILLY Why do you get American when I like Swiss?

LINDA I just thought you'd like a change –

WILLY I don't want a change! I want Swiss cheese. Why am
I always being contradicted?

LINDA (*with a covering laugh*) I thought it would be a
surprise.

WILLY Why don't you open a window in here, for God's
sake?

LINDA (*with infinite patience*) They're all open, dear.

WILLY The way they boxed us in here. Bricks and
windows, windows and bricks.

LINDA We should've bought the land next door.

WILLY The street is lined with cars. There's not a breath of
fresh air in the neighbourhood. The grass don't grow
any more, you can't raise a carrot in the backyard.
They should've had a law against apartment houses.
Remember those two beautiful elm trees out there?
When I and Biff hung the swing between them?

LINDA Yeah, like being a million miles from the city.

WILLY They should've arrested the builder for cutting those
down. They massacred the neighbourhood. (*lost*)
More and more I think of those days, Linda. This
time of year it was lilac and wistaria. And then the
peonies would come out, and the daffodils. What a
fragrance in this room!

LINDA Well, after all, people had to move somewhere.

WILLY No, there's more people now.

LINDA I don't think there's more people, I think –

WILLY There's more people! That's what's ruining this
country! Population is getting out of control. The

competition is maddening! Smell the stink from that apartment house! And another one on the other side ... How can they whip cheese?

On WILLY'S *last line,* BIFF *and* HAPPY *raise themselves up in their beds, listening.*

LINDA Go down, try it. And be quiet.

WILLY (*turning to* LINDA, *guiltily*) You're not worried about me, are you, sweetheart?

BIFF What's the matter?

HAPPY Listen!

LINDA You've got too much on the ball to worry about.

WILLY You're my foundation and my support, Linda.

LINDA Just try to relax, dear. You make mountains out of molehills.

WILLY I won't fight with him any more. If he wants to go back to Texas, let him go.

LINDA He'll find his way.

WILLY Sure. Certain men just don't get started till later in life. Like Thomas Edison, I think. Or B. F. Goodrich. One of them was deaf. (*He starts for the bedroom doorway.*) I'll put my money on Biff.

LINDA And Willy – if it's warm Sunday we'll drive in the country. And we'll open the windshield, and take lunch.

WILLY No, the windshields don't open on the new cars.

LINDA But you opened it today.

WILLY Me? I didn't. (*He stops.*) Now isn't that peculiar! Isn't that a remarkable – (*He breaks off in amazement and fright as the flute is heard distantly.*)

LINDA What, darling?

WILLY That is the most remarkable thing.

LINDA What, dear?

WILLY I was thinking of the Chevvy. (*slight pause*) Nineteen twenty-eight ... when I had that red Chevvy – (*breaks off*) That funny? I coulda sworn I was driving that Chevvy today.

LINDA Well, that's nothing. Something must've reminded you.

WILLY Remarkable. Ts. Remember those days? The way Biff used to simonize that car? The dealer refused to believe there was eighty thousand miles on it. (*He shakes his head.*) Heh! (*To* LINDA.) Close your eyes, I'll be right up. (*He walks out of the bedroom.*)

HAPPY (*to* BIFF) Jesus, maybe he smashed up the car again!

LINDA (*calling after* WILLY) Be careful on the stairs, dear! The cheese is on the middle shelf! (*She turns, goes over to the bed, takes his jacket, and goes out of the bedroom.*) *Light has risen on the boys' room. Unseen,* WILLY *is heard talking to himself,* 'Eighty thousand miles,' *and a little laugh.* BIFF *gets out of bed, comes downstairs a bit, and stands attentively.* BIFF *is two years older than his brother* HAPPY, *well built, but in these days bears a worn air and seems less self-assured. He has succeeded less, and his dreams are stronger and less acceptable than* HAPPY'S. HAPPY *is tall, powerfully made. Sexuality is like a visible colour on him, or a scent that many women have discovered. He, like his brother, is lost, but in a different way, for he has never allowed himself to turn his face toward defeat and is thus more confused and hard-skinned, although seemingly more content.*

HAPPY (*getting out of bed*) He's going to get his licence taken away if he keeps that up. I'm getting nervous about him, y'know, Biff?

BIFF His eyes are going.

HAPPY No, I've driven with him. He sees all right. He just doesn't keep his mind on it. I drove into the city with him last week. He stops at a green light and then it turns red and he goes. (*He laughs.*)

BIFF Maybe he's colour-blind.

HAPPY Pop? Why, he's got the finest eye for colour in the business. You know that.

BIFF (*sitting on his bed*) I'm going to sleep.

HAPPY You're not still sour on Dad, are you, Biff?

BIFF   He's all right, I guess.

WILLY   (*underneath them, in the living-room*) Yes, sir, eighty thousand miles – eighty-two thousand!

BIFF   You smoking?

HAPPY   (*holding out a pack of cigarettes*) Want one?

BIFF   (*taking a cigarette*) I can never sleep when I smell it.

WILLY   What a simonizing job, heh!

HAPPY   (*with deep sentiment*) Funny, Biff, y'know? Us sleeping in here again? The old beds. (*He pats his bed affectionately.*) All the talk that went across those two beds, huh? Our whole lives.

BIFF   Yeah. Lotta dreams and plans.

HAPPY   (*with a deep and masculine laugh*) About five hundred women would like to know what was said in this room.

They share a soft laugh.

BIFF   Remember that big Betsy something – what the hell was her name – over on Bushwick Avenue?

HAPPY   (*combing his hair*) With the collie dog!

BIFF   That's the one. I got you in there, remember?

HAPPY   Yeah, that was my first time – I think. Boy, there was a pig! (*They laugh, almost crudely.*) You taught me everything I know about women. Don't forget that.

BIFF   I bet you forgot how bashful you used to be. Especially with girls.

HAPPY   Oh, I still am, Biff.

BIFF   Oh, go on.

HAPPY   I just control it, that's all. I think I got less bashful and you got more so. What happened, Biff? Where's the old humour, the old confidence? (*He shakes* BIFF'S *knee.* BIFF *gets up and moves restlessly about the room.*) What's the matter?

BIFF   Why does Dad mock me all the time?

HAPPY   He's not mocking you, he –

BIFF   Everything I say there's a twist of mockery on his face. I can't get near him.

HAPPY   He just wants you to make good, that's all. I wanted to talk to you about Dad for a long time, Biff. Something's – happened to him. He – talks to himself.

BIFF   I noticed that this morning. But he always mumbled.

HAPPY   But not so noticeable. It got so embarrassing I sent him to Florida. And you know something? Most of the time he's talking to you.

BIFF   What's he say about me?

HAPPY   I can't make it out.

BIFF   What's he say about me?

HAPPY   I think the fact that you've not settled, that you're still kind of up in the air …

BIFF   There's one or two things depressing him, Happy.

HAPPY   What do you mean?

BIFF   Never mind. Just don't lay it all to me.

HAPPY   But I think if you just got started – I mean – is there any future for you out there?

BIFF   I tell ya, Hap, I don't know what the future is. I don't know – what I'm supposed to want.

HAPPY   What do you mean?

BIFF   Well, I spent six or seven years after high school trying to work myself up. Shipping clerk, salesman, business of one kind or another. And it's a measly manner of existence. To get on that subway on the hot mornings in summer. To devote your whole life to keeping stock, or making phone calls, or selling or buying. To suffer fifty weeks of the year for the sake of a two-week vacation, when all you really desire is to be outdoors, with your shirt off. And always to have to get ahead of the next fella. And still – that's how you build a future.

HAPPY   Well, you really enjoy it on a farm? Are you content out there?

BIFF   (*with rising agitation*) Hap, I've had twenty or thirty different kinds of job since I left home before the war, and it always turns out the same. I just realized it lately. In Nebraska when I herded cattle, and the Dakotas, and Arizona, and now in Texas. It's why I came home now, I guess, because I realized it. This farm I work on, it's spring there now, see? And they've got about fifteen new colts. There's nothing more inspiring or – beautiful than the sight of a mare and a new colt. And it's cool there now, see? Texas is cool now, and it's spring. And whenever spring comes to where I am, I suddenly get the feeling, my God, I'm not gettin' anywhere! What the hell am I doing, playing around with horses, twenty-eight dollars a week! I'm thirty-four years old, I oughta be makin' my future. That's when I come running home. And now, I get here, and I don't know what to do with myself. (*after a pause*) I've always made a point of not wasting my life, and every time I come back here I know that all I've done is to waste my life.

HAPPY   You're a poet, you know that, Biff? You're a – you're an idealist!

BIFF   No, I'm mixed up very bad. Maybe I oughta get married. Maybe I oughta get stuck into something. Maybe that's my trouble. I'm like a boy. I'm not married, I'm not in business, I just – I'm like a boy. Are you content, Hap? You're a success, aren't you? Are you content?

HAPPY   Hell, no!

BIFF   Why? You're making money, aren't you?

HAPPY   (*moving about with energy, expressiveness*) All I can do now is wait for the merchandise manager to die. And suppose I get to be merchandise manager? He's a good friend of mine, and he just built a terrific estate on Long Island. And he lived there about two months and sold it, and now he's building another one. He can't enjoy it once it's finished. And I know that's just what I would do. I don't know what the hell I'm workin' for. Sometimes I sit in my apartment – all alone. And I think of the rent I'm paying. And it's crazy. But then, it's what I always wanted.

My own apartment, a car, and plenty of women. And
still, goddammit, I'm lonely.

BIFF   (*with enthusiasm*) Listen, why don't you come out
West with me?

HAPPY   You and I, heh?

BIFF   Sure, maybe we could buy a ranch. Raise cattle, use
our muscles. Men built like we are should be
working out in the open.

HAPPY   (*avidly*) The Loman Brothers, heh?

BIFF   (*with vast affection*) Sure, we'd be known all over the
counties!

HAPPY   (*enthralled*) That's what I dream about, Biff. Sometimes I want to just rip my clothes off in the middle
of the store and outbox that goddam merchandise
manager. I mean I can outbox, outrun, and outlift
anybody in that store, and I have to take orders from
those common, petty son-of-bitches till I can't stand it
any more.

BIFF   I'm tellin' you, kid, if you were with me I'd be happy
out there.

HAPPY   (*enthused*) See, Biff, everybody around me is so false
that I'm constantly lowering my ideals ...

BIFF   Baby, together we'd stand up for one another, we'd
have someone to trust.

HAPPY   If I were around you –

BIFF   Hap, the trouble is we weren't brought up to grub for
money. I don't know how to do it.

HAPPY   Neither can I!

BIFF   Then let's go!

HAPPY   The only thing is – what can you make out there?

BIFF   But look at your friend. Builds an estate and then
hasn't the peace of mind to live in it.

HAPPY   Yeah, but when he walks into the store the waves
part in front of him. That's fifty-two thousand dollars
a year coming through the revolving door, and I got
more in my pinky finger that he's got in his head.

BIFF Yeah, but you just said –

HAPPY I gotta show some of those pompous, self-important executives over there that Hap Loman can make the grade. I want to walk into the store the way he walks in. Then I'll go with you, Biff. We'll be together yet, I swear. But take those two we had tonight. Now weren't they gorgeous creatures?

BIFF Yeah, yeah, most gorgeous I've had in years.

HAPPY I get that any time I want, Biff. Whenever I feel disgusted. The only trouble is, it gets like bowling or something. I just keep knockin' them over and it doesn't mean anything. You still run around a lot?

BIFF Naa. I'd like to find a girl – steady, somebody with substance.

HAPPY That's what I long for.

BIFF Go on! You'd never come home.

HAPPY I would! Somebody with character, with resistance! Like Mom, y'know? You're gonna call me a bastard when I tell you this. That girl Charlotte I was with tonight is engaged to be married in five weeks. (*He tries on his new hat.*)

BIFF No kiddin'!

HAPPY Sure, the guy's in line for the vice-presidency of the store. I don't know what gets into me; maybe I just have an over-developed sense of competition or something, but I went and ruined her, and furthermore I can't get rid of her. And he's the third executive I've done that to. Isn't that a crummy characteristic? And to top it all, I go to their weddings! (*Indignantly, but laughing.*) Like I'm not supposed to take bribes. Manufacturers offer me a hundred-dollar bill now and then to throw an order their way. You know how honest I am, but it's like this girl, see. I hate myself for it. Because I don't want the girl, and, still, I take it and – I love it!

BIFF Let's go to sleep.

HAPPY I guess we didn't settle anything, heh?

BIFF   I just got one idea that I think I'm going to try.

HAPPY   What's that?

BIFF   Remember Bill Oliver?

HAPPY   Sure, Oliver is very big now. You want to work for him again?

BIFF   No, but when I quit he said something to me. He put his arm on my shoulder, and he said, 'Biff, if you ever need anything, come to me.'

HAPPY   I remember that. That sounds good.

BIFF   I think I'll go and see him. If I could get ten thousand or even seven or eight thousand dollars I could buy a beautiful ranch.

HAPPY   I bet he'd back you. 'Cause he thought highly of you, Biff. I mean, they all do. You're well liked, Biff. That's why I say to come back here, and we both have the apartment. And I'm tellin' you, Biff, any babe you want ...

BIFF   No, with a ranch I could do the work I like and still be something. I just wonder though. I wonder if Oliver still thinks I stole that carton of basketballs.

HAPPY   Oh, he probably forgot that long ago. It's almost ten years. You're too sensitive. Anyway, he didn't really fire you.

BIFF   Well, I think he was going to. I think that's why I quit. I was never sure whether he knew or not. I know he thought the world of me, though. I was the only one he'd let lock up the place.

WILLY   (*below*) You gonna wash the engine, Biff?

HAPPY   Shh!

BIFF *looks at* HAPPY, *who is gazing down, listening.* WILLY *is mumbling in the parlour.*

HAPPY   You hear that?

They listen. WILLY *laughs warmly.*

BIFF   (*growing angry*) Doesn't he know Mom can hear that?

WILLY   Don't you get your sweater dirty, Biff!

A look of pain crosses BIFF's *face.*

HAPPY   Isn't that terrible? Don't leave again, will you? You'll
find a job here. You gotta stick around. I don't
know what to do about him; it's getting
embarrassing.

WILLY   What a simonizing job!

BIFF   Mom's hearing that!

WILLY   No kiddin', Biff, you got a date? Wonderful!

HAPPY   Go on to sleep. But talk to him in the morning, will
you?

BIFF   (*reluctantly getting into bed*) With her in the house.
Brother!

HAPPY   (*getting into bed*) I wish you'd have a good talk
with him.

The light on their room begins to fade.

BIFF   (*to himself in bed*) That selfish, stupid ...

HAPPY   Sh ... Sleep, Biff.

*Their light is out. Well before they have finished
speaking, WILLY'S form is dimly seen below in the
darkened kitchen. He opens the refrigerator, searches
in there, and takes out a bottle of milk. The
apartment houses are fading out, and the entire
house and surroundings become covered with leaves.
Music insinuates itself as the leaves appear.*

WILLY   Just wanna be careful with those girls, Biff, that's all.
Don't make any promises. No promises of any kind.
Because a girl, y'know, they always believe what
you tell 'em, and you're very young, Biff, you're too
young to be talking seriously to girls.

*Light rises on the kitchen. WILLY, talking, shuts the
refrigerator door and comes downstage to the
kitchen table. He pours milk into a glass. He is totally
immersed in himself, smiling faintly.*

WILLY   Too young entirely, Biff. You want to watch your
schooling first. Then when you're all set, there'll be
plenty of girls for a boy like you. (*He smiles broadly
at a kitchen chair.*) That so? The girls pay for you?
(*He laughs.*) Boy, you really must be makin' a hit.

WILLY *is gradually addressing – physically – a point offstage, speaking through the wall of the kitchen, and his voice has been rising in volume to that of a normal conversation.*

WILLY I been wondering why you polish the car so careful. Ha! Don't leave the hubcaps, boys. Get the chamois to the hubcaps. Happy, use newspaper on the windows, it's the easiest thing. Show him how to do it, Biff! You see, Happy? Pad it up, use it like a pad! That's it, that's it, good work. You're doin' all right, Hap. (*He pauses, then nods in approbation for a few seconds, then looks upward.*) Biff, first thing we gotta do when we get time is clip that big branch over the house. Afraid it's gonna fall in a storm and hit the roof. Tell you what. We get a rope and sling her around, and then we climb up there with a couple of saws and take her down. Soon as you finish the car, boys, I wanna see ya. I got a surprise for you, boys.

BIFF (*offstage*) Whatta ya got, Dad?

WILLY No, you finish first. Never leave a job till you're finished – remember that. (*Looking toward the 'big trees'.*) Biff, up in Albany I saw a beautiful hammock. I think I'll buy it next trip, and we'll hang it right between those two elms. Wouldn't that be something? Just swingin' there under those branches. Boy that would …

YOUNG BIFF *and* YOUNG HAPPY *appear from the direction* WILLY *was addressing.* HAPPY *carries rags and a pail of water.* BIFF, *wearing a sweater with a block 'S', carries a football.*

BIFF (*pointing in the direction of the car offstage*) How's that Pop, professional?

WILLY Terrific. Terrific job, boys. Good work, Biff.

HAPPY Where's the surprise, Pop?

WILLY In the back seat of the car.

HAPPY Boy! (*He runs off.*)

BIFF What is it, Dad? Tell me, what'd you buy?

WILLY (*laughing, cuffs him*) Never mind, something I want you to have.

BIFF	(*turns and starts off*) What is it, Hap?
HAPPY	(*offstage*) It's a punching bag!
BIFF	Oh, Pop!
WILLY	It's got Gene Tunney's signature on it!
	HAPPY *runs onstage with a punching bag.*
BIFF	Gee, how'd you know we wanted a punching bag?
WILLY	Well, it's the finest thing for the timing.
HAPPY	(*lies down on his back and pedals with his feet*) I'm losing weight, you notice, Pop?
WILLY	(*to* HAPPY) Jumping rope is good too.
BIFF	Did you see the new football I got?
WILLY	(*examining the ball*) Where'd you get a new ball?
BIFF	The coach told me to practise my passing.
WILLY	That so? And he gave you the ball, heh?
BIFF	Well, I borrowed it from the locker room. (*He laughs confidentially.*)
WILLY	(*laughing with him at the theft*) I want you to return that.
HAPPY	I told you he wouldn't like it!
BIFF	(*angrily*) Well, I'm bringing it back!
WILLY	(*stopping the incipient argument, to* HAPPY) Sure, he's gotta practise with a regulation ball, doesn't he? (*To* BIFF) Coach'll probably congratulate you on your initiative!
BIFF	Oh, he keeps congratulating my initiative all the time, Pop.
WILLY	That's because he likes you. If somebody else took that ball there'd be an uproar. So what's the report, boys, what's the report?
BIFF	Where'd you go this time, Dad? Gee, we were lonesome for you.
WILLY	(*pleased, puts an arm around each boy and they come down to the apron*) Lonesome, heh?
BIFF	Missed you every minute.
WILLY	Don't say? Tell you a secret, boys. Don't breathe it to a soul. Someday I'll have my own business, and I'll never have to leave home any more.

HAPPY Like Uncle Charley, heh?

WILLY Bigger than Uncle Charley! Because Charley is not –
liked. He's liked, but he's not – well liked.

BIFF Where'd you go this time, Dad?

WILLY Well, I got on the road, and I went north to
Providence. Met the Mayor.

BIFF The Mayor of Providence!

WILLY He was sitting in the hotel lobby.

BIFF What'd he say?

WILLY He said, 'Morning!' And I said, 'You got a fine city
here, Mayor.' And then he had coffee with me. And
then I went to Waterbury. Waterbury is a fine city.
Big clock city, the famous Waterbury clock. Sold a
nice bill there. And then Boston – Boston is the
cradle of the Revolution. A fine city. And a couple
of other towns in Mass., and on to Portland and
Bangor and straight home!

BIFF Gee, I'd love to go with you sometime, Dad.

WILLY Soon as summer comes.

HAPPY Promise?

WILLY You and Hap and I, and I'll show you all the towns.
America is full of beautiful towns and fine,
upstanding people. And they know me, boys, they
know me up and down New England. The finest
people. And when I bring you fellas up, there'll be
open sesame for all of us, 'cause one thing, boys: I
have friends. I can park my car in any street in New
England, and the cops protect it like their own. This
summer, heh?

BIFF and **HAPPY** (*together*) Yeah! You bet!

WILLY We'll take your bathing-suits.

HAPPY We'll carry your bags, Pop!

WILLY Oh, won't that be something! Me comin' into the
Boston stores with you two boys carryin' my bags.
What a sensation!

BIFF *is prancing around, practising passing the ball.*

WILLY You nervous, Biff, about the game?

BIFF   Not if you're gonna be there.

WILLY   What do they say about you in school, now that they made you captain?

HAPPY   There's a crowd of girls behind him every time the classes change.

BIFF   (*taking* WILLY'S *hand*) This Saturday, Pop, this Saturday – just for you, I'm going to break through for a touchdown.

HAPPY   You're supposed to pass.

BIFF   I'm takin' one play for Pop. You watch me, Pop, and when I take off my helmet, that means I'm breakin' out. Then watch me crash through that line!

WILLY   (*kisses* BIFF) Oh, wait'll I tell this in Boston!

BERNARD *enters in knickers. He is younger than* BIFF, *earnest and loyal, a worried boy.*

BERNARD   Biff, where are you? You're supposed to study with me today.

WILLY   Hey, looka Bernard. What're you lookin' so anaemic about, Bernard?

BERNARD   He's gotta study, Uncle Willy. He's got Regents next week.

HAPPY   (*tauntingly, spinning* BERNARD *around*) Let's box, Bernard!

BERNARD   Biff! (*He gets away from* HAPPY.) Listen, Biff, I heard Mr Birnbaum say that if you don't start studyin' math he's gonna flunk you, and you won't graduate. I heard him!

WILLY   You better study with him, Biff. Go ahead now.

BERNARD   I heard him!

BIFF   Oh, Pop, you didn't see my sneakers! (*He holds up a foot for* WILLY *to look at.*)

WILLY   Hey, that's a beautiful job of printing!

BERNARD   (*wiping his glasses*) Just because he printed University of Virginia on his sneakers doesn't mean they've got to graduate him, Uncle Willy!

WILLY   (*angrily*) What're you talking about? With scholarships to three universities they're gonna flunk him?

BERNARD	But I heard Mr Birnbaum say –
WILLY	Don't be a pest, Bernard! (*to his boys*) What an anaemic!
BERNARD	Okay, I'm waiting for you in my house, Biff.
	BERNARD *goes off.* *The* LOMANS *laugh.*
WILLY	Bernard is not well liked, is he?
BIFF	He's liked, but he's not well liked.
HAPPY	That's right, Pop.
WILLY	That's just what I mean. Bernard can get the best marks in school, y'understand, but when he gets out in the business world, y'understand, you are going to be five times ahead of him. That's why I thank Almighty God you're both built like Adonises. Because the man who makes an appearance in the business world, the man who creates personal interest, is the man who gets ahead. Be liked and you will never want. You take me, for instance. I never have to wait in line to see a buyer. 'Willy Loman is here!' That's all they have to know, and I go right through.
BIFF	Did you knock them dead, Pop?
WILLY	Knocked 'em cold in Providence, slaughtered 'em in Boston.
HAPPY	(*on his back, pedalling again*) I'm losing weight, you notice, Pop?
	LINDA *enters, as of old, a ribbon in her hair, carrying a basket of washing.*
LINDA	(*with youthful energy*) Hello, dear!
WILLY	Sweetheart!
LINDA	How'd the Chevvy run?
WILLY	Chevrolet, Linda, is the greatest car ever built. (*to the boys*) Since when do you let your mother carry wash up the stairs?
BIFF	Grab hold there, boy!
HAPPY	Where to, Mom?
LINDA	Hang them up on the line. And you better go down

to your friends, Biff. The cellar is full of boys. They
don't know what to do with themselves.

BIFF Ah, when Pop comes home they can wait!

WILLY (*laughs appreciatively*) You better go down and tell
them what to do, Biff.

BIFF I think I'll have them sweep out the furnace room.

WILLY Good work, Biff.

BIFF (*goes through wall-line of kitchen to doorway at back
and calls down*) Fellas! Everybody sweep out the
furnace room! I'll be right down!

VOICES All right! Okay, Biff.

BIFF George and Sam and Frank, come out back! We're
hangin' up the wash! Come on, Hap, on the double!
(*He and* HAPPY *carry out the basket.*)

LINDA The way they obey him!

WILLY Well, that's training, the training. I'm tellin' you, I was
sellin' thousands and thousands, but I had to come
home.

LINDA Oh, the whole block'll be at the game. Did you sell
anything?

WILLY I did five hundred gross in Providence and seven
hundred gross in Boston.

LINDA No! Wait a minute, I've got a pencil. (*She pulls pencil
and paper out of her apron pocket.*) That makes your
commission ... Two hundred – my God! Two
hundred and twelve dollars!

WILLY Well, I didn't figure it yet, but ...

LINDA How much did you do?

WILLY Well, I – I did – about a hundred and eighty gross in
Providence. Well, no – it came to – roughly two
hundred gross on the whole trip.

LINDA (*without hesitation*) Two hundred gross. That's ...
She figures.

WILLY The trouble was that three of the stores were half-
closed for inventory in Boston. Otherwise I woulda
broke records.

LINDA   Well, it makes seventy dollars and some pennies. That's very good.

WILLY   What do we owe?

LINDA   Well, on the first there's sixteen dollars on the refrigerator –

WILLY   Why sixteen?

LINDA   Well, the fan belt broke, so it was a dollar eighty.

WILLY   But it's brand new.

LINDA   Well, the man said that's the way it is. Till they work themselves in, y'know.

They move through the wall-line into the kitchen.

WILLY   I hope we didn't get stuck on that machine.

LINDA   They got the biggest ads of any of them!

WILLY   I know, it's a fine machine. What else?

LINDA   Well, there's nine-sixty for the washing-machine. And for the vacuum cleaner there's three and a half due on the fifteenth. Then the roof, you got twenty-one dollars remaining.

WILLY   It don't leak, does it?

LINDA   No, they did a wonderful job. Then you owe Frank for the carburettor.

WILLY   I'm not going to pay that man! That goddam Chevrolet, they ought to prohibit the manufacture of that car!

LINDA   Well, you owe him three and a half. And odds and ends, comes to around a hundred and twenty dollars by the fifteenth.

WILLY   A hundred and twenty dollars! My God, if business don't pick up I don't know what I'm gonna do!

LINDA   Well, next week you'll do better.

WILLY   Oh, I'll knock 'em dead next week. I'll go to Hartford. I'm very well liked in Hartford. You know, the trouble is, Linda, people don't seem to take to me.

They move on to the forestage.

LINDA   Oh, don't be foolish.

WILLY   I know it when I walk in. They seem to laugh at me.

LINDA   Why? Why would they laugh at you? Don't talk that way, Willy.

WILLY moves to the edge of the stage. LINDA *goes into the kitchen and starts to darn stockings.*

WILLY   I don't know the reason for it, but they just pass me by. I'm not noticed.

LINDA   But you're doing wonderful, dear. You're making seventy to a hundred dollars a week.

WILLY   But I gotta be at it ten, twelve hours a day. Other men – I don't know – they do it easier. I don't know why – I can't stop myself – I talk too much. A man oughta come in with a few words. One thing about Charley. He's a man of few words, and they respect him.

LINDA   You don't talk too much, you're just lively.

WILLY   (*smiling*) Well, I figure, what the hell, life is short, a couple of jokes. (*To himself.*) I joke too much! (*The smile goes.*)

LINDA   Why? You're –

WILLY   I'm fat. I'm very – foolish to look at, Linda. I didn't tell you, but Christmas-time I happened to be calling on F. H. Stewarts, and a salesman I know, as I was going in to see the buyer I heard him say something about – walrus. And I – I cracked him right across the face. I won't take that. I simply will not take that. But they do laugh at me. I know that.

LINDA   Darling …

WILLY   I gotta overcome it. I know I gotta overcome it. I'm not dressing to advantage, maybe.

LINDA   Willy, darling, you're the handsomest man in the world –

WILLY   Oh, no, Linda.

LINDA   To me you are. (*Slight pause.*) The handsomest.
From the darkness is heard the laughter of a woman.
WILLY *doesn't turn to it, but it continues through* LINDA'S *lines.*

LINDA   And the boys, Willy. Few men are idolized by their children the way you are.

Music is heard behind a scrim, to the left of the house. The WOMAN, *dimly seen, is dressing.*

WILLY   (*with great feeling*) You're the best there is, Linda, you're a pal, you know that? On the road – on the road I want to grab you sometimes and just kiss the life outa you.

The laughter is loud now, and he moves into a brightening area at the left, where the WOMAN *has come from behind the scrim and is standing, putting on her hat, looking into a 'mirror', and laughing.*

WILLY   'Cause I get so lonely – especially when business is bad and there's nobody to talk to. I get the feeling that I'll never sell anything again, that I won't make a living for you, or a business, a business for the boys. (*He talks through the* WOMAN'S *subsiding laughter. The* WOMAN *primps at the 'mirror'.*) There's so much I want to make for –

THE WOMAN   Me? You didn't make me, Willy. I picked you.

WILLY   (*pleased*) You picked me?

THE WOMAN   (*who is quite proper-looking,* WILLY'S *age*) I did. I've been sitting at that desk watching all the salesmen go by, day in, day out. But you've got such a sense of humour, and we do have such a good time together, don't we?

WILLY   Sure, sure. (*He takes her in his arms.*) Why do you have to go now?

THE WOMAN   It's two o'clock …

WILLY   No, come on in! (*He pulls her.*)

THE WOMAN   … my sisters'll be scandalized. When'll you be back?

WILLY   Oh, two weeks about. Will you come up again?

THE WOMAN   Sure thing. You do make me laugh. It's good for me. (*She squeezes his arm, kisses him.*) And I think you're a wonderful man.

WILLY   You picked me, heh?

THE WOMAN	Sure. Because you're so sweet. And such a kidder.
WILLY	Well, I'll see you next time I'm in Boston.
THE WOMAN	I'll put you right through to the buyers.
WILLY	(*slapping her bottom*) Right. Well, bottoms up!
THE WOMAN	(*slaps him gently and laughs*) You just kill me, Willy. (*He suddenly grabs her and kisses her roughly.*) You kill me. And thanks for the stockings. I love a lot of stockings. Well, good night.
WILLY	Good night. And keep your pores open!
THE WOMAN	Oh, Willy!

The WOMAN *bursts out laughing, and* LINDA'S *laughter blends in. The* WOMAN *disappears into the dark. Now the area at the kitchen table brightens.* LINDA *is sitting where she was at the kitchen table, but now is mending a pair of her silk stockings.*

LINDA	You are, Willy. The handsomest man. You've got no reason to feel that –
WILLY	(*coming out of the* WOMAN'S *dimming area and going over to* LINDA) I'll make it all up to you, Linda, I'll –
LINDA	There's nothing to make up, dear. You're doing fine, better than –
WILLY	(*noticing her mending*) What's that?
LINDA	Just mending my stockings. They're so expensive –
WILLY	(*angrily, taking them from her*) I won't have you mending stockings in this house! Now throw them out!

LINDA *puts the stockings in her pocket.*

BERNARD	(*entering on the run*) Where is he? If he doesn't study!
WILLY	(*moving to the forestage, with great agitation*) You'll give him the answers!
BERNARD	I do, but I can't on a Regents! That's a state exam! They're liable to arrest me!
WILLY	Where is he? I'll whip him, I'll whip him!
LINDA	And he'd better give back that football, Willy; it's not nice.
WILLY	Biff! Where is he? Why is he taking everything?

LINDA	He's too rough with the girls, Willy. All the mothers are afraid of him!
WILLY	I'll whip him!
BERNARD	He's driving the car without a licence!
	The WOMAN's *laugh is heard.*
WILLY	Shut up!
LINDA	All the mothers –
WILLY	Shut up!
BERNARD	(*backing quietly away and out*) Mr Birnbaum says he's stuck up.
WILLY	Get outa here!
BERNARD	If he doesn't buckle down he'll flunk math! (*He goes off.*)
LINDA	He's right, Willy, you've gotta –
WILLY	(*exploding at her*) There's nothing the matter with him! You want him to be a worm like Bernard? He's got spirit, personality …
	As he speaks, LINDA, *almost in tears, exits into the living-room.* WILLY *is alone in the kitchen, wilting and staring. The leaves are gone. It is night again, and the apartment houses look down from behind.*
WILLY	Loaded with it. Loaded! What is he stealing? He's giving it back, isn't he? Why is he stealing? What did I tell him? I never in my life told him anything but decent things.
	HAPPY *in pyjamas has come down the stairs;* WILLY *suddenly becomes aware of* HAPPY's *presence.*
HAPPY	Let's go now, come on.
WILLY	(*sitting down at the kitchen table*) Huh! Why did she have to wax the floors herself? Every time she waxes the floors she kneels over. She knows that!
HAPPY	Shh! Take it easy. What brought you back tonight?
WILLY	I got an awful scare. Nearly hit a kid in Yonkers. God! Why didn't I go to Alaska with my brother Ben that time! Ben! That man was a genius, that man was success incarnate! What a mistake! He begged me to go.

HAPPY	Well, there's no use in –
WILLY	You guys! There was a man started with the clothes on his back and ended up with diamond mines!
HAPPY	Boy, someday I'd like to know how he did it.
WILLY	What's the mystery! The man knew what he wanted and went out and got it! Walked into a jungle, and comes out, the age of twenty-one, and he's rich! The world is an oyster, but you don't crack it open on a mattress!
HAPPY	Pop, I told you I'm gonna retire you for life.
WILLY	You'll retire me for life on seventy goddam dollars a week? And your women and your car and your apartment, and you'll retire me for life! Christ's sake, I couldn't get past Yonkers today! Where are you guys, where are you? The woods are burning! I can't drive a car!
	CHARLEY *has appeared in the doorway. He is a large man, slow of speech, laconic, immovable. In all he says, despite what he says, there is pity, and, now, trepidation. He has a robe over pyjamas, slippers on his feet. He enters the kitchen.*
CHARLEY	Everything all right?
HAPPY	Yeah, Charley, everything's …
WILLY	What's the matter?
CHARLEY	I heard some noise. I thought something happened. Can't we do something about the walls? You sneeze in here, and in my house hats blow off.
HAPPY	Let's go to bed, Dad. Come on.
	CHARLEY *signals* HAPPY *to go.*
WILLY	You go ahead, I'm not tired at the moment.
HAPPY	(*to* WILLY) Take it easy, huh? (*He exits.*)
WILLY	What're you doin' up?
CHARLEY	(*sitting down at the kitchen table opposite* WILLY) Couldn't sleep good. I had a heartburn.
WILLY	Well, you don't know how to eat.
CHARLEY	I eat with my mouth.
WILLY	No, you're ignorant. You gotta know about vitamins and things like that.

CHARLEY	Come on, let's shoot. Tire you out a little.
WILLY	(*hesitantly*) All right. You got cards?
CHARLEY	(*taking a deck from his pocket*) Yeah, I got them. Someplace. What is it with those vitamins?
WILLY	(*dealing*) They build up your bones. Chemistry.
CHARLEY	Yeah, but there's no bones in a heartburn.
WILLY	What are you talkin' about? Do you know the first thing about it?
CHARLEY	Don't get insulted.
WILLY	Don't talk about something you don't know anything about.
	They are playing. Pause.
CHARLEY	What're you doin' home?
WILLY	A little trouble with the car.
CHARLEY	Oh. (*Pause.*) I'd like to take a trip to California.
WILLY	Don't say.
CHARLEY	You want a job?
WILLY	I got a job, I told you that. (*After a slight pause.*) What the hell are you offering me a job for?
CHARLEY	Don't get insulted.
WILLY	Don't insult me.
CHARLEY	I don't see no sense in it. You don't have to go on this way.
WILLY	I got a good job. (*Slight pause.*) What do you keep comin' in here for?
CHARLEY	You want me to go?
WILLY	(*after a pause, withering*) I can't understand it. He's going back to Texas again. What the hell is that?
CHARLEY	Let him go.
WILLY	I got nothin' to give him, Charley, I'm clean, I'm clean.
CHARLEY	He won't starve. None of them starve. Forget about him.
WILLY	Then what have I got to remember?
CHARLEY	You take it too hard. To hell with it. When a deposit bottle is broken you don't get your nickel back.

WILLY That's easy enough for you to say.

CHARLEY That ain't easy for me to say.

WILLY Did you see the ceiling I put in the living-room?

CHARLEY Yeah, that's a piece of work. To put up a ceiling is a mystery to me. How do you do it?

WILLY What's the difference?

CHARLEY Well, talk about it.

WILLY You gonna put up a ceiling?

CHARLEY How could I put up a ceiling?

WILLY Then what the hell are you bothering me for?

CHARLEY You're insulted again.

WILLY A man who can't handle tools is not a man. You're disgusting.

CHARLEY Don't call me disgusting, Willy.

UNCLE BEN, *carrying a valise and an umbrella, enters the forestage from around the right corner of the house. He is a stolid man, in his sixties, with a moustache and an authoritative air. He is utterly certain of his destiny, and there is an aura of far places about him. He enters exactly as* WILLY *speaks.*

WILLY I'm getting awfully tired, Ben.

BEN'S *music is heard.* BEN *looks around at everything.*

CHARLEY Good, keep playing; you'll sleep better. Did you call me Ben?

BEN *looks at his watch.*

WILLY That's funny. For a second there you reminded me of my brother Ben.

BEN I only have a few minutes. (*He strolls, inspecting the place.* WILLY *and* CHARLEY *continue playing.*)

CHARLEY You never heard from him again, heh? Since that time?

WILLY Didn't Linda tell you? Couple of weeks ago we got a letter from his wife in Africa. He died.

CHARLEY That so.

BEN (*chuckling*) So this is Brooklyn, eh?

CHARLEY Maybe you're in for some of his money.

WILLY	Naa, he had seven sons. There's just one opportunity I had with that man …
BEN	I must make a train, William. There are several properties I'm looking at in Alaska.
WILLY	Sure, sure! If I'd gone with him to Alaska that time, everything would've been totally different.
CHARLEY	Go on, you'd froze to death up there.
WILLY	What're you talking about?
BEN	Opportunity is tremendous in Alaska, William. Surprised you're not up there.
WILLY	Sure, tremendous.
CHARLEY	Heh?
WILLY	There was the only man I ever met who knew the answers.
CHARLEY	Who?
BEN	How are you all?
WILLY	(*taking a pot, smiling*) Fine, fine.
CHARLEY	Pretty sharp tonight.
BEN	Is Mother living with you?
WILLY	No, she died a long time ago.
CHARLEY	Who?
BEN	That's too bad. Fine specimen of a lady, Mother.
WILLY	(*to* CHARLEY) Heh?
BEN	I'd hoped to see the old girl.
CHARLEY	Who died?
BEN	Heard anything from Father, have you?
WILLY	(*unnerved*) What do you mean, who died?
CHARLEY	(*taking a pot*) What're you talkin' about?
BEN	(*looking at his watch*) William, it's half past eight!
WILLY	(*as though to dispel his confusion he angrily stops* CHARLEY'S *hand*) That's my build!
CHARLEY	I put the ace –
WILLY	If you don't know how to play the game I'm not gonna throw my money away on you!
CHARLEY	(*rising*) It was my ace, for God's sake!

WILLY	I'm through, I'm through!
BEN	When did Mother die?
WILLY	Long ago. Since the beginning you never knew how to play cards.
CHARLEY	(*picks up the cards and goes to the door*) All right! Next time I'll bring a deck with five aces.
WILLY	I don't play that kind of game!
CHARLEY	(*turning to him*) You ought to be ashamed of yourself!
WILLY	Yeah?
CHARLEY	Yeah! (*He goes out.*)
WILLY	(*slamming the door after him*) Ignoramus!
BEN	(*as* WILLY *comes towards him through the wall-line of the kitchen*) So you're William.
WILLY	(*shaking* BEN'S *hand*) Ben! I've been waiting for you so long! What's the answer? How did you do it?
BEN	Oh, there's a story in that.
	LINDA *enters the forestage, as of old, carrying the wash basket.*
LINDA	Is this Ben?
BEN	(*gallantly*) How do you do, my dear?
LINDA	Where've you been all these years? Willy's always wondered why you –
WILLY	(*pulling* BEN *away from her impatiently*) Where is Dad? Didn't you follow him? How did you get started?
BEN	Well, I don't know how much you remember.
WILLY	Well, I was just a baby, of course, only three or four years old –
BEN	Three years and eleven months.
WILLY	What a memory, Ben!
BEN	I have many enterprises, William, and I have never kept books.
WILLY	I remember I was sitting under the wagon in – was it Nebraska?
BEN	It was South Dakota, and I gave you a bunch of wild flowers.

WILLY	I remember you walking away down some open road.
BEN	(*laughing*) I was going to find Father in Alaska.
WILLY	Where is he?
BEN	At that age I had a very faulty view of geography, William. I discovered after a few days that I was heading due south, so instead of Alaska, I ended up in Africa.
LINDA	Africa!
WILLY	The Gold Coast!
BEN	Principally diamond mines.
LINDA	Diamond mines!
BEN	Yes, my dear. But I've only a few minutes –
WILLY	No! Boys! Boys! (YOUNG BIFF *and* HAPPY *appear.*) Listen to this. This is your Uncle Ben, a great man! Tell my boys, Ben!
BEN	Why, boys, when I was seventeen I walked into the jungle, and when I was twenty-one I walked out. (*He laughs.*) And by God I was rich.
WILLY	(*to the boys*) You see what I been talking about? The greatest things can happen!
BEN	(*glancing at his watch*) I have an appointment in Ketchikan Tuesday week.
WILLY	No, Ben! Please tell about Dad. I want my boys to hear. I want them to know the kind of stock they spring from. All I remember is a man with a big beard, and I was in Mamma's lap, sitting around a fire, and some kind of high music.
BEN	His flute. He played the flute.
WILLY	Sure, the flute, that's right!
	New music is heard, a high, rollicking tune.
BEN	Father was a very great and a very wild-hearted man. We would start in Boston, and he'd toss the whole family into the wagon, and then he'd drive the team right across the country; through Ohio, and Indiana, Michigan, Illinois, and all the Western states. And we'd stop in the towns and

sell the flutes that he'd made on the way. Great
inventor, Father. With one gadget he made more in a
week than a man like you could make in a lifetime.

WILLY That's just the way I'm bringing them up, Ben –
rugged, well liked, all-around.

BEN Yeah? (*To* BIFF) Hit that, boy – hard as you can. (*He
pounds his stomach.*)

BIFF Oh, no, sir!

BEN (*taking boxing stance*) Come on, get to me! (*He
laughs.*)

WILLY Go to it, Biff! Go ahead, show him!

BIFF Okay! (*He cocks his fists and starts in.*)

LINDA (*to* WILLY) Why must he fight, dear?

BEN (*sparring with* BIFF) Good boy! Good boy!

WILLY How's that, Ben, heh?

HAPPY Give him the left, Biff!

LINDA Why are you fighting?

BEN Good boy! (*Suddenly comes in, trips* BIFF, *and stands
over him, the point of his umbrella poised over* BIFF'S
eye.)

LINDA Look out, Biff!

BIFF Gee!

BEN (*patting* BIFF'S *knee*) Never fight fair with a stranger,
boy. You'll never get out of the jungle that way.
(*Taking* LINDA'S *hand and bowing.*) It was an honour
and a pleasure to meet you, Linda.

LINDA (*withdrawing her hand, coldly, frightened*) Have a
nice – trip.

BEN (to WILLY) And good luck with your – what do you do?

WILLY Selling.

BEN Yes. Well … (*He raises his hand in farewell to all.*)

WILLY No, Ben, I don't want you to think … (*He takes* BEN'S *arm
to show him.*) It's Brooklyn, I know, but we hunt too.

BEN Really, now.

WILLY Oh, sure, there's snakes and rabbits and – that's why
I moved out here. Why, Biff can fell any one of these
trees in no time! Boys! Go right over to where they're

building the apartment house and get some sand. We're gonna rebuild the entire front stoop right now! Watch this, Ben!

BIFF Yes, sir! On the double, Hap!

HAPPY (*as he and* BIFF *run off*) I lost weight, Pop, you notice? CHARLEY *enters in knickers, even before the boys are gone.*

CHARLEY Listen, if they steal any more from that building the watchman'll put the cops on them!

LINDA (*to* WILLY) Don't let Biff ...
BEN *laughs lustily.*

WILLY You shoulda seen the lumber they brought home last week. At least a dozen six-by-tens worth all kinds a money.

CHARLEY Listen, if that watchman –

WILLY I gave them hell, understand. But I got a couple of fearless characters there.

CHARLEY Willy, the jails are full of fearless characters.

BEN (*clapping* WILLY *on the back, with a laugh at* CHARLEY) And the stock exchange, friend!

WILLY (*joining in* BEN'S *laughter*) Where are the rest of your pants?

CHARLEY My wife brought them.

WILLY Now all you need is a golf club and you can go upstairs and go to bed. (*To* BEN) Great athlete! Between him and his son Bernard they can't hammer a nail!

BERNARD (*rushing in*) The watchman's chasing Biff!

WILLY (*angrily*) Shut up! He's not stealing anything!

LINDA (*alarmed, hurrying off left*) Where is he? Biff, dear! *She exits.*

WILLY (*moving toward the left, away from* BEN) There's nothing wrong. What's the matter with you?

BEN Nervy boy. Good!

WILLY (*laughing*) Oh, nerves of iron, that Biff!

CHARLEY Don't know what it is. My New England man comes back and he's bleedin'; they murdered him up there.

WILLY   It's contacts, Charley, I got important contacts!

CHARLEY (*sarcastically*) Glad to hear it, Willy. Come in later, we'll shoot a little casino. I'll take some of your Portland money. (*He laughs at* WILLY *and exits.*)

WILLY   (*turning to* BEN) Business is bad, it's murderous. But not for me, of course.

BEN   I'll stop by on my way back to Africa.

WILLY   (*longingly*) Can't you stay a few days? You're just what I need, Ben, because I – I have a fine position here, but I – well, Dad left when I was such a baby and I never had a chance to talk to him and I still feel – kind of temporary about myself.

BEN   I'll be late for my train.

They are at opposite ends of the stage.

WILLY   Ben, my boys – can't we talk? They'd go into the jaws of hell for me, see but I –

BEN   William, you're being first-rate with your boys. Outstanding, manly chaps!

WILLY   (*hanging on to his words*) Oh, Ben, that's good to hear! Because sometimes I'm afraid that I'm not teaching them the right kind of – Ben, how should I teach them?

BEN   (*giving great weight to each word, and with a certain vicious audacity*) William, when I walked into the jungle, I was seventeen. When I walked out I was twenty-one. And, by God, I was rich! (*He goes off into darkness around the right corner of the house.*)

WILLY   ... was rich! That's just the spirit I want to imbue them with! To walk into a jungle! I was right! I was right! I was right!

BEN is gone, but WILLY *is still speaking to him as* LINDA, *in nightgown and robe, enters the kitchen, glances around for* WILLY, *then goes to the door of the house, looks out and sees him. Comes down to his left. He looks at her.*

LINDA   Willy, dear? Willy?

WILLY   I was right!

LINDA　Did you have some cheese? (*He can't answer.*) It's very late, darling. Come to bed, heh?

WILLY　(*looking straight up*) Gotta break your neck to see a star in this yard.

LINDA　You coming in?

WILLY　Whatever happened to that diamond watch fob? Remember? When Ben came from Africa that time? Didn't he give me a watch fob with a diamond in it?

LINDA　You pawned it, dear. Twelve, thirteen years ago. For Biff's radio correspondence course.

WILLY　Gee, that was a beautiful thing. I'll take a walk.

LINDA　But you're in your slippers.

WILLY　(*starting to go around the house at the left*) I was right! I was! (*Half to* LINDA, *as he goes, shaking his head.*) What a man! There was a man worth talking to. I was right!

LINDA　(*calling after* WILLY) But in your slippers, Willy!
　　　　WILLY is almost gone when BIFF, *in his pyjamas, comes down the stairs and enters the kitchen.*

BIFF　What is he doing out there?

LINDA　Sh!

BIFF　God Almighty, Mom, how long has he been doing this?

LINDA　Don't, he'll hear you.

BIFF　What the hell is the matter with him?

LINDA　It'll pass by morning.

BIFF　Shouldn't we do anything?

LINDA　Oh, my dear, you should do a lot of things, but there's nothing to do, so go to sleep.
　　　　HAPPY *comes down the stairs and sits on the steps.*

HAPPY　I never heard him so loud, Mom.

LINDA　Well, come around more often; you'll hear him.
　　　　She sits at the table and mends the lining of WILLY'S *jacket.*

BIFF　Why didn't you ever write me about this, Mom?

LINDA　How would I write to you? For over three months you had no address.

BIFF   I was on the move. But you know I thought of you all the time. You know that, don't you, pal?

LINDA   I know, dear, I know. But he likes to have a letter. Just to know that there's still a possibility for better things.

BIFF   He's not like this all the time, is he?

LINDA   It's when you come home he's always the worst.

BIFF   When I come home?

LINDA   When you write you're coming, he's all smiles, and talks about the future, and – he's just wonderful. And then the closer you seem to come, the more shaky he gets, and then, by the time you get here, he's arguing, and he seems angry at you. I think it's just that maybe he can't bring himself to – to open up to you. Why are you so hateful to each other? Why is it?

BIFF   (*evasively*) I'm not hateful, Mom.

LINDA   But you no sooner come in the door than you're fighting!

BIFF   I don't understand why. I mean to change. I'm tryin', Mom; you understand?

LINDA   Are you home to stay now?

BIFF   I don't know. I want to look around, see what's doin'.

LINDA   Biff, you can't look around all your life, can you?

BIFF   I just can't take hold, Mom. I can't take hold of some kind of a life.

LINDA   Biff, a man is not a bird, to come and go with the springtime.

BIFF   Your hair … (*He touches her hair.*) Your hair got so grey.

LINDA   Oh, it's been grey since you were in high school. I just stopped dyeing it, that's all.

BIFF   Dye it again, will ya? I don't want my pal looking old. (*He smiles.*)

LINDA   You're such a boy! You think you can go away for a year and … You've got to get it into your head now that one day you'll knock on this door and there'll be strange people here —

BIFF   What are you talking about? You're not even sixty
Mom.

LINDA   But what about your father?

BIFF   (*lamely*) Well, I meant him too.

HAPPY   He admires Pop.

LINDA   Biff, dear, if you don't have any feeling for him,
then you can't have any feeling for me.

BIFF   Sure I can, Mom.

LINDA   No. You can't just come to see me, because I love
him. (*With a threat, but only a threat, of tears.*) He's
the dearest man in the world to me, and I won't have
anyone making him feel unwanted and low and
blue. You've got to make up your mind now, darling,
there's no leeway any more. Either he's your father
and you pay him that respect, or else you're not to
come here. I know he's not easy to get along with –
nobody knows that better than me – but ...

WILLY   (*from the left, with a laugh*) Hey, hey, Biffo!

BIFF   (*starting to go out after* WILLY) What the hell is the
matter with him? (HAPPY s*tops him.*)

LINDA   Don't – don't go near him!

BIFF   Stop making excuses for him! He always, always
wiped the floor with you. Never had an ounce of
respect for you.

HAPPY   He's always had respect for —

BIFF   What the hell do you know about it?

HAPPY   (*surlily*) Just don't call him crazy!

BIFF   He's got no character – Charley wouldn't do this.
Not in his own house – spewing out that vomit from
his mind.

HAPPY   Charley never had to cope with what he's got to.

BIFF   People are worse off than Willy Loman. Believe me,
I've seen them.

LINDA   Then make Charley your father, Biff. You can't
do that, can you? I don't say he's a great man.
Willy Loman never made a lot of money. His
name was never in the paper. He's not the finest
character that ever lived. But he's a human
being, and a terrible thing is happening to him.

So attention must be paid. He's not to be allowed to fall into his grave like an old dog. Attention, attention must be finally paid to such a person. You called him crazy —

BIFF I didn't mean —

LINDA No, a lot of people think he's lost his – balance. But you don't have to be very smart to know what his trouble is. The man is exhausted.

HAPPY Sure!

LINDA A small man can be just as exhausted as a great man. He works for a company thirty-six years this March, opens up unheard-of territories to their trademark, and now in his old age they take his salary away.

HAPPY (*indignantly*) I didn't know that, Mom.

LINDA You never asked, my dear! Now that you get your spending money someplace else you don't trouble your mind with him.

HAPPY But I gave you money last —

LINDA Christmas-time, fifty dollars! To fix the hot water it cost ninety-seven fifty! For five weeks he's been on straight commission, like a beginner, an unknown!

BIFF Those ungrateful bastards!

LINDA Are they any worse than his sons? When he brought them business, when he was young, they were glad to see him. But now his old friends, the old buyers that loved him so and always found some order to hand him in a pinch – they're all dead, retired. He used to be able to make six, seven calls a day in Boston. Now he takes his valises out of the car and puts them back and takes them out again and he's exhausted. Instead of walking he talks now. He drives seven hundred miles, and when he gets there no one knows him any more, no one welcomes him. And what goes through a man's mind, driving seven hundred miles home without having earned a cent? Why shouldn't he talk to himself? Why? When he has to go to Charley and borrow fifty dollars a week and pretend to me that it's his pay? How

long can that go on? How long? You see what I'm
sitting here and waiting for? And you tell me he has
no character? The man who never worked a day but
for your benefit? When does he get the medal for
that? Is this his reward – to turn around at the age of
sixty-three and find his sons, who he loved better
than his life, one a philandering bum –

HAPPY   Mom!

LINDA   That's all you are, my baby! (*To* BIFF) And you! What
happened to the love you had for him? You were
such pals! How you used to talk to him on the
phone every night! How lonely he was till he could
come home to you!

BIFF   All right, Mom. I'll live here in my room, and I'll get
a job. I'll keep away from him, that's all.

LINDA   No, Biff. You can't stay here and fight all the time.

BIFF   He threw me out of this house, remember that.

LINDA   Why did he do that? I never knew why.

BIFF   Because I know he's a fake and he doesn't like
anybody around who knows!

LINDA   Why a fake! In what way? What do you mean?

BIFF   Just don't lay it all at my feet. It's between me and
him – that's all I have to say. I'll chip in from now
on. He'll settle for half my pay cheque. He'll be all
right. I'm going to bed. (*He starts for the stairs.*)

LINDA   He won't be all right.

BIFF   (*turning on the stairs, furiously*) I hate this city and
I'll stay here. Now what do you want?

LINDA   He's dying, Biff.

HAPPY *turns quickly to her, shocked.*

BIFF   (*after a pause*) Why is he dying?

LINDA   He's been trying to kill himself.

BIFF   (*with great horror*) How?

LINDA   I live from day to day.

BIFF   What're you talking about?

LINDA   Remember I wrote you that he smashed up the car
again? In February?

BIFF   Well?

LINDA   The insurance inspector came. He said that they have evidence. That all these accidents in the last year – weren't – weren't – accidents.

HAPPY   How can they tell that? That's a lie.

LINDA   It seems there's a woman ... (*She takes a breath as*)

BIFF   (*sharply but contained*)   What woman?

LINDA   (*simultaneously*)   ... and this woman ...

LINDA   What?

BIFF   Nothing. Go ahead.

LINDA   What did you say?

BIFF   Nothing. I just said what woman?

HAPPY   What about her?

LINDA   Well, it seems she was walking down the road and saw his car. She says that he wasn't driving fast at all, and that he didn't skid. She says he came to that little bridge, and then deliberately smashed into the railing, and it was only the shallowness of the water that saved him.

BIFF   Oh, no, he probably just fell asleep again.

LINDA   I don't think he fell asleep.

BIFF   Why not?

LINDA   Last month ... (*with great difficulty*) Oh, boy, it's so hard to say a thing like this! He's just a big stupid man to you, but I tell you there's more good in him than in many other people. (*She chokes, wipes her eyes.*) I was looking for a fuse. The lights blew out, and I went down the cellar. And behind the fuse-box – it happened to fall out – was a length of rubber pipe – just short.

HAPPY   No kidding?

LINDA   There's a little attachment on the end of it. I knew right away. And sure enough, on the bottom of the water heater there's a new little nipple on the gas pipe.

HAPPY   (*angrily*) That – jerk.

BIFF   Did you have it taken off!

LINDA   I'm – I'm ashamed to. How can I mention it to him?

Every day I go down and take away the little rubber pipe. But, when he comes home, I put it back where it was. How can I insult him that way? I don't know what to do. I live from day to day, boys. I tell you, I know every thought in his mind. It sounds so old-fashioned and silly, but I tell you he put his whole life into you and you've turned your backs on him. (*She is bent over in the chair, weeping, her face in her hands.*) Biff, I swear to God! Biff, his life is in your hands!

HAPPY (*to* BIFF) How do you like that damned fool!

BIFF (*kissing her*) All right, pal, all right. It's all settled now. I've been remiss. I know that, Mom. But now I'll stay, and I swear to you, I'll apply myself. (*Kneeling in front of her, in a fever of self-reproach.*) It's just – you see, Mom, I don't fit in business. Not that I won't try. I'll try, and I'll make good.

HAPPY Sure you will. The trouble with you in business was you never tried to please people.

BIFF I know, I —

HAPPY Like when you worked for Harrison's. Bob Harrison said you were tops, and then you go and do some damn fool thing like whistling whole songs in the elevator like a comedian.

BIFF (*against* HAPPY) So what? I like to whistle sometimes.

HAPPY You don't raise a guy to a responsible job who whistles in the elevator!

LINDA Well, don't argue about it now.

HAPPY Like when you'd go off and swim in the middle of the day instead of taking the line around.

BIFF (*his resentment rising*) Well, don't you run off? You take off sometimes, don't you? On a nice summer day?

HAPPY Yeah, but I cover myself!

LINDA Boys!

HAPPY If I'm going to take a fade the boss can call any number where I'm supposed to be and they'll swear to him that I just left. I'll tell you something that I hate to say, Biff, but in the business world some of them think you're crazy.

BIFF (*angered*) Screw the business world!

HAPPY All right, screw it! Great, but cover yourself!

LINDA Hap, Hap!

BIFF I don't care what they think! They've laughed at Dad for years, and you know why? Because we don't belong in this nuthouse of a city! We should be mixing cement on some open plain, or – or carpenters. A carpenter is allowed to whistle!

WILLY *walks in from the entrance of the house, at left.*

WILLY Even your grandfather was better than a carpenter. (*Pause. They watch him.*) You never grew up. Bernard does not whistle in the elevator, I assure you.

BIFF (*as though to laugh* WILLY *out of it*) Yeah, but you do, Pop.

WILLY I never in my life whistled in an elevator! And who in the business world thinks I'm crazy?

BIFF I didn't mean it like that, Pop. Now don't make a whole thing out of it, will ya?

WILLY Go back to the West! Be a carpenter, a cowboy, enjoy yourself!

LINDA Willy, he was just saying —

WILLY I heard what he said!

HAPPY (*trying to quiet* WILLY) Hey, Pop, come on now ...

WILLY (*continuing over* HAPPY's *line*) They laugh at me, heh? Go to Filene's, go to the Hub, go to Slattery's, Boston. Call out the name Willy Loman and see what happens! Big shot!

BIFF All right, Pop.

WILLY Big!

BIFF All right!

WILLY Why do you always insult me?

BIFF I didn't say a word. (*to* LINDA) Did I say a word?

LINDA He didn't say anything, Willy.

WILLY (*going to the doorway of the living-room*) All right, good night, good night.

LINDA   Willy, dear, he just decided ...

WILLY   (*to* BIFF) If you get tired hanging around tomorrow, paint the ceiling I put up in the living-room.

BIFF   I'm leaving early tomorrow.

HAPPY   He's going to see Bill Oliver, Pop.

WILLY   (*interestedly*) Oliver? For what?

BIFF   (*with reserve, but trying, trying*) He always said he'd stake me. I'd like to go into business, so maybe I can run him up on it.

LINDA   Isn't that wonderful?

WILLY   Don't interrupt. What's wonderful about it? There's fifty men in the City of New York who'd stake him. (*To* BIFF) Sporting goods?

BIFF   I guess so. I know something about it and —

WILLY   He knows something about it! You know sporting goods better than Spalding, for God's sake! How much is he giving you?

BIFF   I don't know, I didn't even see him yet, but —

WILLY   Then what're you talkin' about?

BIFF   (*getting angry*) Well, all I said was I'm gonna see him, that's all!

WILLY   (*turning away*) Ah, you're counting your chickens again.

BIFF   (*starting left for the stairs*) Oh, Jesus, I'm going to sleep!

WILLY   (*calling after him*) Don't curse in this house!

BIFF   (*turning*) Since when did you get so clean?

HAPPY   (*trying to stop them*) Wait a ...

WILLY   Don't use that language to me! I won't have it!

HAPPY   (*grabbing* BIFF, *shouts*) Wait a minute! I got an idea. I got a feasible idea. Come here, Biff, let's talk this over now, let's talk some sense here. When I was down in Florida last time, I thought of a great idea to sell sporting goods. It just came back to me. You and I, Biff – we have a line, the Loman Line. We train a couple of weeks, and put on a couple of exhibitions, see?

WILLY That's an idea!

HAPPY Wait! We form two basketball teams, see? Two water-polo teams. We play each other. It's a million dollars' worth of publicity. Two brothers, see? The Loman Brothers. Displays in the Royal Palms – all the hotels. And banners over the ring and the basketball court: 'Loman Brothers'. Baby, we could sell sporting goods!

WILLY That is a one-million-dollar idea!

LINDA Marvellous!

BIFF I'm in great shape as far as that's concerned.

HAPPY And the beauty of it is, Biff, it wouldn't be like a business. We'd be out playin' ball again ...

BIFF (*enthused*) Yeah, that's ...

WILLY Million-dollar ...

HAPPY And you wouldn't get fed up with it, Biff. It'd be the family again. There'd be the old honour, and comradeship, and if you wanted to go off for a swim or somethin' – well, you'd do it! Without some smart cooky gettin' up ahead of you!

WILLY Lick the world! You guys together could absolutely lick the civilized world.

BIFF I'll see Oliver tomorrow. Hap, if we could work that out ...

LINDA Maybe things are beginning to —

WILLY (*wildy enthused, to* LINDA) Stop interrupting. (*To* BIFF.) But don't wear sport jacket and slacks when you see Oliver.

BIFF No, I'll —

WILLY A business suit, and talk as little as possible, and don't crack any jokes.

BIFF He did like me. Always liked me.

LINDA He loved you!

WILLY (*to* LINDA) Will you stop! (*To* BIFF.) Walk in very serious. You are not applying for a boy's job. Money is to pass. Be quiet, fine, and serious. Everybody likes a kidder, but nobody lends him money.

HAPPY   I'll try to get some myself, Biff. I'm sure I can.

WILLY   I see great things for you kids, I think your troubles are over. But remember, start big and you'll end big. Ask for fifteen. How much you gonna ask for?

BIFF   Gee, I don't know —

WILLY   And don't say 'Gee'. 'Gee' is a boy's word. A man walking in for fifteen thousand dollars does not say 'Gee'!

BIFF   Ten, I think, would be top though.

WILLY   Don't be so modest. You always started too low. Walk in with a big laugh. Don't look worried. Start off with a couple of good stories to lighten things up. It's not what you say, it's how you say it – because personality always wins the day.

LINDA   Oliver always thought the highest of him —

WILLY   Will you let me talk?

BIFF   Don't yell at her, Pop, will ya?

WILLY   (*angrily*) I was talking, wasn't I?

BIFF   I don't like you yelling at her all the time, and I'm tellin' you, that's all.

WILLY   What're you, takin' over this house?

LINDA   Willy —

WILLY   (*turning on her*) Don't take his side all the time, goddammit!

BIFF   (*furiously*) Stop yelling at her!

WILLY   (*suddenly pulling on his cheek, beaten down, guilt ridden*) Give my best to Bill Oliver – he may remember me. (*He exits through the living-room doorway.*)

LINDA   (*her voice subdued*) What'd you have to start that for? (BIFF *turns away.*) You see how sweet he was as soon as you talked hopefully? (*She goes over to* BIFF.) Come up and say good night to him. Don't let him go to bed that way.

HAPPY   Come on, Biff, let's buck him up.

LINDA   Please, dear. Just say good night. It takes so little to make him happy. Come. (*She goes through the living-room doorway,* *calling upstairs from within the living-room.*) Your pyjamas are hanging in the bathroom, Willy!

HAPPY (*looking toward where* LINDA *went out*) What a woman! They broke the mould when they made her. You know that, Biff?

BIFF He's off salary. My God, working on commission!

HAPPY Well, let's face it: he's no hot-shot selling man. Except that sometimes, you have to admit, he's a sweet personality.

BIFF (*deciding*) Lend me ten bucks, will ya! I want to buy some new ties.

HAPPY I'll take you to a place I know. Beautiful stuff. Wear one of my striped shirts tomorrow.

BIFF She got grey. Mom got awful old. Gee. I'm gonna go in to Oliver tomorrow and knock him for a —

HAPPY Come on up. Tell that to Dad. Let's give him a whirl. Come on.

BIFF (*steamed up*) You know, with ten thousand bucks, boy!

HAPPY (*as they go into the living-room*) That's the talk, Biff, that's the first time I've heard the old confidence out of you! (*From within the living-room, fading off.*) You're gonna live with me, kid, and any babe you want, just say the word ... (*The last lines are hardly heard. They are mounting the stairs to their parents' bedroom.*)

LINDA (*entering her bedroom and addressing* WILLY, *who is in the bathroom. She is straightening the bed for him.*) Can you do anything about the shower? It drips.

WILLY (*from the bathroom*) All of a sudden everything falls to pieces! Goddam plumbing, oughta be sued, those people. I hardly finished putting it in and the thing ... (*His words rumble off.*)

LINDA I'm just wondering if Oliver will remember him. You think he might?

WILLY (*coming out of the bathroom in his pyjamas*) Remember him? What's the matter with you, you crazy? If he'd've stayed with Oliver he'd be on top by now! Wait'll Oliver gets a look at him. You don't know the average calibre any more. The average young man today – (*he is getting into bed*) – is got a calibre of zero. Greatest thing in the world for him was to bum around.

BIFF *and* HAPPY *enter the bedroom. Slight pause.*

WILLY (*stops short, looking at* BIFF) Glad to hear it, boy.

HAPPY He wanted to say good night to you, sport.

WILLY (*to* BIFF) Yeah. Knock him dead, boy. What'd you want to tell me?

BIFF Just take it easy, Pop. Good night. (*He turns to go.*)

WILLY (*unable to resist*) And if anything falls off the desk while you're talking to him – like a package or something – don't you pick it up. They have office boys for that.

LINDA I'll make a big breakfast —

WILLY Will you let me finish? (*To* BIFF) Tell him you were in the business in the West. Not farm work.

BIFF All right, Dad.

LINDA I think everything —

WILLY (*going right through her speech*) And don't undersell yourself. No less than fifteen thousand dollars.

BIFF (*unable to bear him*) Okay. Good night, Mom. (*He starts moving.*)

WILLY Because you got a greatness in you, Biff, remember that. You got all kinds a greatness ... (*He lies back, exhausted.* BIFF *walks out.*)

LINDA (*calling after* BIFF) Sleep well, darling!

HAPPY I'm gonna get married, Mom. I wanted to tell you.

LINDA Go to sleep, dear.

HAPPY (*going*) I just wanted to tell you.

WILLY Keep up the good work. (HAPPY *exits.*) God ... remember that Ebbets Field game? The championship of the city?

LINDA Just rest. Should I sing to you?

WILLY Yeah. Sing to me. (LINDA *hums a soft lullaby*.) When that team came out – he was the tallest, remember?

LINDA Oh, yes. And in gold.

BIFF *enters the darkened kitchen, takes a cigarette, and leaves the house. He comes downstage into a golden pool of light. He smokes, staring at the night.*

WILLY Like a young god. Hercules – something like that. And the sun, the sun all around him. Remember how he waved to me? Right up from the field, with the representatives of three colleges standing by? And the buyers I brought, and the cheers when he came out – Loman, Loman, Loman! God Almighty, he'll be great yet. A star like that, magnificent, can never really fade away!

The light on WILLY *is fading. The gas heater begins to glow through the kitchen wall, near the stairs, a blue flame beneath red coils.*

LINDA (*timidly*) Willy dear, what has he got against you?

WILLY I'm so tired. Don't talk any more.

BIFF *slowly returns to the kitchen. He stops, stares toward the heater.*

LINDA Will you ask Howard to let you work in New York?

WILLY First thing in the morning. Everything'll be all right.

BIFF *reaches behind the heater and draws out a length of rubber tubing. He is horrified and turns his head toward* WILLY'S *room, still dimly lit, from which the strains of* LINDA'S *desperate but monotonous humming rise.*

WILLY (*staring through the window into the moonlight*) Gee, look at the moon moving between the buildings!

BIFF *wraps the tubing around his hand and quickly goes up the stairs.*

CURTAIN

ACT TWO

*Music is heard, gay and bright. The curtain rises as
the music fades away.*

WILLY, *in shirt sleeves, is sitting at the kitchen table,
sipping coffee, his hat on his lap.* LINDA *is filling his
cup when she can.*

WILLY Wonderful coffee. Meal in itself.

LINDA Can I make you some eggs?

WILLY No. Take a breath.

LINDA You look so rested, dear.

WILLY I slept like a dead one. First time in months.
Imagine, sleeping till ten on a Tuesday morning.
Boys left nice and early, heh?

LINDA They were out of here by eight o'clock.

WILLY Good work!

LINDA It was so thrilling to see them leaving together. I
can't get over the shaving lotion in this house!

WILLY (*smiling*) Mmm —

LINDA Biff was very changed this morning. His whole
attitude seemed to be hopeful. He couldn't wait to
get downtown to see Oliver.

WILLY He's heading for a change. There's no question,
there simply are certain men that take longer to get
– solidified. How did he dress?

LINDA His blue suit. He's so handsome in that suit. He
could be a – anything in that suit!

WILLY *gets up from the table.* LINDA *holds the jacket for
him.*

WILLY There's no question, no question at all. Gee, on the
way home tonight I'd like to buy some seeds.

LINDA (*laughing*) That'd be wonderful. But not enough sun gets back there. Nothing'll grow any more.

WILLY You wait, kid, before it's all over we're gonna get a little place out in the country, and I'll raise some vegetables, a couple of chickens ...

LINDA You'll do it yet, dear.

WILLY *walks out of his jacket.* LINDA *follows him.*

WILLY And they'll get married, and come for a weekend. I'd build a little guest house, 'Cause I got so many fine tools, all I'd need would be a little lumber and some peace of mind.

LINDA (*joyfully*) I sewed the lining ...

WILLY I could build two guest houses, so they'd both come. Did he decide how much he's going to ask Oliver for?

LINDA (*getting him into the jacket*) He didn't mention it, but I imagine ten or fifteen thousand. You going to talk to Howard today?

WILLY Yeah. I'll put it to him straight and simple. He'll just have to take me off the road.

LINDA And Willy, don't forget to ask for a little advance, because we've got the insurance premium. It's the grace period now.

WILLY That's a hundred ...?

LINDA A hundred and eight, sixty-eight. Because we're a little short again.

WILLY Why are we short?

LINDA Well, you had the motor job on the car ...

WILLY That goddam Studebaker!

LINDA And you got one more payment on the refrigerator ...

WILLY But it just broke again!

LINDA Well, it's old, dear.

WILLY I told you we should've bought a well-advertised machine. Charley bought a General Electric and it's twenty years old and it's still good, that son-of-a-bitch.

LINDA But, Willy —

WILLY   Whoever heard of a Hastings refrigerator? Once in my life I would like to own something outright before it's broken! I'm always in a race with the junkyard! I just finished paying for the car and it's on its last legs. The refrigerator consumes belts like a goddam maniac. They time those things. They time them so when you finally paid for them, they're used up.

LINDA   (*buttoning up his jacket as he unbuttons it*) All told, about two hundred dollars would carry us, dear. But that includes the last payment on the mortgage. After this payment, Willy, the house belongs to us.

WILLY   It's twenty-five years!

LINDA   Biff was nine years old when we bought it.

WILLY   Well, that's a great thing. To weather a twenty-five-year mortgage is —

LINDA   It's an accomplishment.

WILLY   All the cement, the lumber, the reconstruction I put in this house! There ain't a crack to be found in it any more.

LINDA   Well, it served its purpose.

WILLY   What purpose? Some stranger'll come along, move in, and that's that. If only Biff would take this house, and raise a family ... (*He starts to go.*) Good-bye, I'm late.

LINDA   (*suddenly remembering*) Oh, I forgot! You're supposed to meet them for dinner.

WILLY   Me?

LINDA   At Frank's Chop House on Forty-eighth near Sixth Avenue.

WILLY   Is that so! How about you?

LINDA   No, just the three of you. They're gonna blow you to a big meal!

WILLY   Don't say! Who thought of that?

LINDA   Biff came to me this morning, Willy, and he said, 'Tell Dad, we want to blow him to a big meal.' Be there six o'clock. You and your two boys are going to have dinner.

WILLY   Gee whiz! That's really somethin'. I'm gonna knock

Howard for a loop, kid. I'll get an advance, and I'll come home with a New York job. Goddammit, now I'm gonna do it!

LINDA   Oh, that's the spirit, Willy!

WILLY   I will never get behind a wheel the rest of my life!

LINDA   It's changing, Willy, I can feel it changing!

WILLY   Beyond a question. G'bye, I'm late. (*He starts to go again.*)

LINDA   (*calling after him as she runs to the kitchen table for a handkerchief*) You got your glasses?

WILLY   (*feels for them, then comes back in*) Yeah, yeah, got my glasses.

LINDA   (*giving him the handkerchief*) And a handkerchief.

WILLY   Yeah, handkerchief.

LINDA   And your saccharine?

WILLY   Yeah, my saccharine.

LINDA   Be careful on the subway stairs.

She kisses him, and a silk stocking is seen hanging from her hand. WILLY *notices it.*

WILLY   Will you stop mending stockings? At least while I'm in the house. It gets me nervous. I can't tell you. Please.

LINDA *hides the stockings in her hand as she follows* WILLY *across the stage in front of the house.*

LINDA   Remember, Frank's Chop House.

WILLY   (*passing the apron*) Maybe beets would grow out there.

LINDA   (*laughing*) But you tried so many times.

WILLY   Yeah. Well, don't work hard today. (*He disappears around the right corner of the house.*)

LINDA   Be careful!

As WILLY *vanishes,* LINDA *waves to him. Suddenly the phone rings. She runs across the stage and into the kitchen and lifts it.*

LINDA   Hello? Oh, Biff! I'm so glad you called, I just ... Yes, sure, I just told him. Yes, he'll be there for dinner at six o'clock. I didn't forget. Listen, I was just dying to tell you. You know that little rubber pipe I told you about? That he connected to the gas heater? I finally decided to go down the cellar this morning and take it away and destroy it. But it's gone! Imagine! He took it away himself, it isn't there! (*She listens.*) When? Oh, then you took it. Oh – nothing, it's just that I'd hoped he'd taken it away himself. Oh, I'm not worried, darling, because this morning he left in such high spirits, it was like the old days! I'm not afraid any more. Did Mr Oliver see you? ... Well, you wait there then. And make a nice impression on him, darling. Just don't perspire too much before you see him. And have a nice time with Dad. He may have big news too! ... That's right, a New York job. And be sweet to him tonight, dear. Be loving to him. Because he's only a little boat looking for a harbour. (*She is trembling with sorrow and joy.*) Oh, that's wonderful, Biff, you'll save his life. Thanks, darling. Just put your arm around him when he comes into the restaurant. Give him a smile. That's the boy ... Good-bye, dear ... You got your comb? ... That's fine. Good-bye, Biff dear.

In the middle of her speech, HOWARD WAGNER, *thirty-six, wheels on a small typewriter table on which is a wire-recording machine and proceeds to plug it in. This is on the left forestage. Light slowly fades on* LINDA *as it rises on* HOWARD. HOWARD *is intent on threading the machine and only glances over his shoulder as* WILLY *appears.*

WILLY   Pst! Pst!

HOWARD   Hello, Willy, come in.

WILLY   Like to have a little talk with you, Howard.

HOWARD   Sorry to keep you waiting. I'll be with you in a minute.

WILLY   What's that, Howard?

HOWARD   Didn't you ever see one of these? Wire recorder.

WILLY   Oh. Can we talk a minute?

HOWARD   Records things. Just got delivery yesterday. Been

driving me crazy, the most terrific machine I ever
saw in my life. I was up all night with it.

WILLY What do you do with it?

HOWARD I bought it for dictation, but you can do anything
with it. Listen to this. I had it home last night. Listen
to what I picked up. The first one is my daughter.
Get this. (*He flicks the switch and 'Roll out the
Barrel' is heard being whistled.*) Listen to that kid
whistle.

WILLY That is lifelike, isn't it?

HOWARD Seven years old. Get that tone.

WILLY Ts, ts. Like to ask a little favour if you ...
The whistling breaks off, and the voice of HOWARD'S
DAUGHTER *is heard.*

HIS DAUGHTER   'Now you, Daddy.'

HOWARD She's crazy for me! (*Again the same song is
whistled.*) That's me! Ha! (*He winks.*)

WILLY You're very good!
*The whistling breaks off again. The machine runs
silent for a moment.*

HOWARD Sh! Get this now, this is my son.

HIS SON 'The capital of Alabama is Montgomery; the
capital of Arizona is Phoenix; the capital of
Arkansas is Little Rock; the capital of California is
Sacramento ...' (*and on, and on.*)

HOWARD (*holding up five fingers*) Five years old, Willy!

WILLY He'll make an announcer some day!

HIS SON (*continuing*) 'The capital ...'

HOWARD Get that – alphabetical order! (*The machine breaks
off suddenly.*) Wait a minute. The maid kicked the
plug out.

WILLY It certainly is a —

HOWARD Sh, for God's sake!

HIS SON 'It's nine o'clock. Bulova watch time. So I have to
go to sleep.'

WILLY That really is —

HOWARD	Wait a minute! The next is my wife.
	They wait.
HOWARD'S VOICE	'Go on, say something.' (*Pause.*) 'Well, you gonna talk?'
HIS WIFE	'I can't think of anything.'
HOWARD'S VOICE	'Well, talk – it's turning.'
HIS WIFE	(*shyly, beaten*) 'Hello.' (*Silence.*) 'Oh, Howard, I can't talk into this ...'
HOWARD	(*snapping the machine off*) That was my wife.
WILLY	That is a wonderful machine. Can we —
HOWARD	I tell you, Willy, I'm gonna take my camera, and my bandsaw, and all my hobbies, and out they go. This is the most fascinating relaxation I ever found.
WILLY	I think I'll get one myself.
HOWARD	Sure, they're only a hundred and a half. You can't do without it. Supposing you wanna hear Jack Benny, see? But you can't be at home at that hour. So you tell the maid to turn the radio on when Jack Benny comes on, and this automatically goes on with the radio ...
WILLY	And when you come home you ...
HOWARD	You can come home twelve o'clock, one o'clock, any time you like, and you get yourself a Coke and sit yourself down, throw the switch, and there's Jack Benny's programme in the middle of the night!
WILLY	I'm definitely going to you get one. Because lots of time I'm on the road, and I think to myself, what I must be missing on the radio!
HOWARD	Don't you have a radio in the car?
WILLY	Well, yeah, but who ever thinks of turning it on?
HOWARD	Say, aren't you supposed to be in Boston?
WILLY	That's what I want to talk to you about, Howard. You got a minute? (*He draws a chair in from the wing.*)
HOWARD	What happened? What're you doing here?
WILLY	Well ...

HOWARD   You didn't crack up again, did you?

WILLY   Oh, no. No ...

HOWARD   Geez, you had me worried there for a minute. What's the trouble?

WILLY   Well, tell you the truth, Howard. I've come to the decision that I'd rather not travel any more.

HOWARD   Not travel! Well, what'll you do?

WILLY   Remember, Christmas-time, when you had the party here? You said you'd try to think of some spot for me here in town.

HOWARD   With us?

WILLY   Well, sure.

HOWARD   Oh, yeah, yeah. I remember. Well, I couldn't think of anything for you, Willy.

WILLY   I tell ya, Howard. The kids are all grown up, y'know. I don't need much any more. If I could take home – well, sixty-five dollars a week, I could swing it.

HOWARD   Yeah, but Willy, see I —

WILLY   I tell ya why, Howard. Speaking frankly and between the two of us, y'know – I'm just a little tired.

HOWARD   Oh, I could understand that, Willy. But you're a road man, Willy, and we do a road business. We've only got a half-dozen salesmen on the floor here.

WILLY   God knows, Howard, I never asked a favour of any man. But I was with the firm when your father used to carry you here in his arms.

HOWARD   I know that, Willy, but —

WILLY   Your father came to me the day you were born and asked me what I thought of the name of Howard, may he rest in peace.

HOWARD   I appreciate that, Willy, but there just is no spot here for you. If I had a spot I'd slam you right in, but I just don't have a single solitary spot.

          He looks for his lighter. WILLY *has picked it up and gives it to him. Pause.*

WILLY   (*with increasing anger*) Howard, all I need to set my table is fifty dollars a week.

HOWARD   But where am I going to put you, kid?

WILLY   Look, it isn't a question of whether I can sell merchandise, is it?

HOWARD   No, but it's a business, kid, and everybody's gotta pull his own weight.

WILLY   (*desperately*) Just let me tell you a story, Howard —

HOWARD   'Cause you gotta admit, business is business.

WILLY   (*angrily*) Business is definitely business, but just listen for a minute. You don't understand this. When I was a boy – eighteen, nineteen – I was already on the road. And there was a question in my mind as to whether selling had a future for me. Because in those days I had a yearning to go to Alaska. See, there were three gold strikes in one month in Alaska, and I felt like going out. Just for the ride, you might say.

HOWARD   (*barely interested*) Don't say.

WILLY   Oh, yeah, my father lived many years in Alaska. He was an adventurous man. We've got quite a little streak of self-reliance in our family. I thought I'd go out with my older brother and try to locate him and maybe settle in the North with the old man. And I was almost decided to go, when I met a salesman in the Parker House. His name was Dave Singleman. And he was eighty-four years old, and he'd drummed merchandise in thirty-one states. And old Dave, he'd go up to his room, y'understand, put on his green velvet slippers – I'll never forget – and pick up his phone and call the buyers, and without ever leaving his room, at the age of eighty-four, he made his living. And when I saw that, I realized that selling was the greatest career a man could want. 'Cause what could be more satisfying than to be able to go, at the age of eighty-four, into twenty or thirty different cities, and pick up a phone, and be remembered and loved and helped by so many different people?

Do you know? when he died – and by the way, he
died the death of a salesman, in his green velvet
slippers in the smoker of the New York, New Haven,
and Hartford, going into Boston – when he died,
hundreds of salesmen and buyers were at his funeral.
Things were sad on a lotta trains for months after
that. (*He stands up.* HOWARD *has not looked at him.*) In
those days there was personality in it, Howard. There
was respect, and comradeship, and gratitude in it.
Today, it's all cut and dried, and there's no chance
for bringing friendship to bear – or personality. You
see what I mean? They don't know me any more.

HOWARD (*moving away, toward the right*) That's just the
thing, Willy.

WILLY If I had forty dollars a week – that's all I'd need.
Forty dollars, Howard.

HOWARD Kid, I can't take blood from a stone, I —

WILLY (*desperation is on him now*) Howard, the year Al
Smith was nominated, your father came to me and —

HOWARD (*starting to go off*) I've got to see some people, kid.

WILLY (*stopping him*) I'm talking about your father! There
were promises made across this desk! You mustn't
tell me you've got people to see – I put thirty-four
years into this firm, Howard, and now I can't pay
my insurance! You can't eat the orange and throw
the peel away – a man is not a piece of fruit! (*after
a pause*) Now pay attention. Your father – in 1928 I
had a big year. I averaged a hundred and seventy
dollars a week in commissions.

HOWARD (*impatiently*) Now, Willy, you never averaged —

WILLY (*banging his hand on the desk*) I averaged a
hundred and seventy dollars a week in the year of
1928! And your father came to me – or rather, I was
in the office here – it was right over this desk – and
he put his hand on my shoulder —

HOWARD (*getting up*) You'll have to excuse me, Willy, I gotta
see some people. Pull yourself together. (*going out*)
I'll be back in a little while.

On HOWARD'S *exit, the light on his chair grows very bright and strange.*

WILLY Pull yourself together! What the hell did I say to him? My God, I was yelling at him! How could I! (WILLY *breaks off, staring at the light, which occupies the chair, animating it. He approaches this chair, standing across the desk from it.*) Frank, Frank, don't you remember what you told me that time? How you put your hand on my shoulder, and Frank ... (*He leans on the desk and as he speaks the dead man's name he accidentally switches on the recorder, and instantly —*)

HOWARD'S SON '... of New York is Albany. The capital of Ohio is Cincinnati, the capital of Rhode Island is ...' (*The recitation continues.*)

WILLY (*leaping away in fright, shouting*) Ha! Howard! Howard! Howard!

HOWARD (*rushing in*) What happened?

WILLY (*pointing to the machine, which continues nasally, childishly, with the capital cities*) Shut it off! Shut it off!

HOWARD (*pulling the plug out*) Look, Willy ...

WILLY (*pressing his hands to his eyes*) I gotta get myself some coffee. I'll get some coffee ...

WILLY *starts to walk out.* HOWARD *stops him.*

HOWARD (*rolling up the cord*) Willy, look ...

WILLY I'll go to Boston.

HOWARD Willy, you can't go to Boston for us.

WILLY Why can't I go?

HOWARD I don't want you to represent us. I've been meaning to tell you for a long time now.

WILLY Howard, are you firing me?

HOWARD I think you need a good long rest, Willy.

WILLY Howard —

HOWARD And when you feel better, come back, and we'll see if we can work something out.

WILLY But I gotta earn money, Howard. I'm in no position to —

HOWARD	Where are your sons? Why don't your sons give you a hand?
WILLY	They're working on a very big deal.
HOWARD	This is no time for false pride, Willy. You go to your sons and you tell them that you're tired. You've got two great boys, haven't you?
WILLY	Oh, no question, no question, but in the meantime ...
HOWARD	Then that's that, heh?
WILLY	All right, I'll go to Boston tomorrow.
HOWARD	No, no.
WILLY	I can't throw myself on my sons. I'm not a cripple!
HOWARD	Look, kid, I'm busy this morning.
WILLY	(*grasping* HOWARD'S *arm*) Howard, you've got to let me go to Boston!
HOWARD	(*hard, keeping himself under control*) I've got a line of people to see this morning. Sit down, take five minutes, and pull yourself together, and then go home, will ya? I need the office, Willy. (*He starts to go, turns, remembering the recorder, starts to push off the table holding the recorder.*) Oh, yeah. Whenever you can this week, stop by and drop off the samples. You'll feel better, Willy, and then come back and we'll talk. Pull yourself together, kid, there's people outside.

HOWARD *exits, pushing the table off left.* WILLY *stares into space, exhausted. Now the music is heard –* BEN'S *music – first distantly, then closer, closer. As* WILLY *speaks,* BEN *enters from the right. He carries valise and umbrella.*

WILLY	Oh, Ben, how did you do it? What is the answer? Did you wind up the Alaska deal already?
BEN	Doesn't take much time if you know what you're doing. Just a short business trip. Boarding ship in an hour. Wanted to say good-bye.
WILLY	Ben, I've got to talk to you.
BEN	(*glancing at his watch*) Haven't the time, William.

WILLY   (*crossing the apron to* BEN) Ben, nothing's working out. I don't know what to do.

BEN   Now, look here, William. I've bought timberland in Alaska and I need a man to look after things for me.

WILLY   God, timberland! Me and my boys in those grand outdoors!

BEN   You've a new continent at your doorstep, William. Get out of these cities, they're full of talk and time payments and courts of law. Screw on your fists and you can fight for a fortune up there.

WILLY   Yes, yes! Linda, Linda!

          LINDA *enters as of old, with the wash.*

LINDA   Oh, you're back?

BEN   I haven't much time.

WILLY   No, wait! Linda, he's got a proposition for me in Alaska.

LINDA   But you've got – (*to* BEN) He's got a beautiful job here.

WILLY   But in Alaska, kid, I could —

LINDA   You're doing well enough, Willy!

BEN   (*to* LINDA) Enough for what, my dear?

LINDA   (*frightened of* BEN *and angry at him*) Don't say those things to him! Enough to be happy right here, right now. (*to* WILLY, *while* BEN *laughs*) Why must everybody conquer the world? You're well liked, and the boys love you, and someday – (*to* BEN) – why, old man Wagner told him just the other day that if he keeps it up he'll be a member of the firm, didn't he, Willy?

WILLY   Sure, sure. I am building something with this firm, Ben, and if a man is building something he must be on the right track, mustn't he?

BEN   What are you building? Lay your hand on it. Where is it?

WILLY   (*hesitantly*) That's true, Linda, there's nothing.

LINDA   Why? (*to* BEN) There's a man eighty-four years old —

WILLY That's right, Ben, that's right. When I look at that man I say, what is there to worry about?

BEN Bah!

WILLY It's true, Ben. All he has to do is go into any city, pick up the phone, and he's making his living and you know why?

BEN (*picking up his valise*) I've got to go.

WILLY (*holding* BEN *back*) Look at this boy!

BIFF, *in his high-school sweater, enters carrying suitcase.* HAPPY *carries* BIFF's *shoulder guards, gold helmet, and football pants.*

WILLY Without a penny to his name, three great universities are begging for him, and from there the sky's the limit, because it's not what you do, Ben. It's who you know and the smile on your face! It's contacts, Ben, contacts! The whole wealth of Alaska passes over the lunch table at the Commodore Hotel, and that's the wonder, the wonder of this country, that a man can end with diamonds here on the basis of being liked! (*He turns to* BIFF.) And that's why when you get out on that field today it's important. Because thousands of people will be rooting for you and loving you. (*To* BEN, *who has again begun to leave.*) And Ben! when he walks into a business office his name will sound out like a bell and all the doors will open to him! I've seen it, Ben, I've seen it a thousand times! You can't feel it with your hand like timber, but it's there!

BEN Good-bye, William.

WILLY Ben, am I right? Don't you think I'm right? I value your advice.

BEN There's a new continent at your doorstep, William. You could walk out rich. Rich! (*He is gone.*)

WILLY We'll do it here, Ben! You hear me? We're gonna do it here!

Young BERNARD *rushes in. The gay music of the boys is heard.*

BERNARD Oh, gee, I was afraid you left already!

WILLY Why? What time is it?

BERNARD It's half past one!

WILLY Well, come on, everybody! Ebbets Field next stop! Where's the pennants? (*He rushes through the wall-line of the kitchen and out in to the living-room.*)

LINDA (*to* BIFF) Did you pack fresh underwear?

BIFF (*who has been limbering up*) I want to go!

BERNARD Biff, I'm carrying your helmet, ain't I?

HAPPY No, I'm carrying the helmet.

BERNARD Oh, Biff, you promised me.

HAPPY I'm carrying the helmet.

BERNARD How am I going to get in the locker room?

LINDA Let him carry the shoulder guards. (*She puts her coat and hat on in the kitchen.*)

BERNARD Can I, Biff? 'Cause I told everybody I'm going to be in the locker room.

HAPPY In Ebbets Field it's the clubhouse.

BERNARD I meant the clubhouse. Biff!

HAPPY Biff!

BIFF (*grandly, after a slight pause*) Let him carry the shoulder guards.

HAPPY (*as he gives* BERNARD *the shoulder guards*) Stay close to us now.

WILLY *rushes in with the pennants.*

WILLY (*handing them out*) Everybody wave when Biff comes out on the field. (HAPPY *and* BERNARD *run off.*) You set now, boys?

The music has died away.

BIFF Ready to go, Pop. Every muscle is ready.

WILLY (*at the edge of the apron*) You realize what this means?

BIFF That's right, Pop.

WILLY (*feeling* BIFF'S *muscles*) You're comin' home this afternoon captain of the All-Scholastic Championship Team of the City of New York.

BIFF   I got it, Pop. And remember, pal, when I take off my helmet, that touchdown is for you.

WILLY   Let's go! (*He is starting out, with his arm around* BIFF, *when* CHARLEY *enters, as of old, in knickers.*) I got no room for you, Charley.

CHARLEY Room? For what?

WILLY   In the car.

CHARLEY You goin' for a ride? I wanted to shoot some casino.

WILLY   (*furiously*) Casino! (*Incredulously.*) Don't you realize what today is?

LINDA   Oh, he knows, Willy. He's just kidding you.

WILLY   That's nothing to kid about!

CHARLEY No, Linda, what's goin' on?

LINDA   He's playing in Ebbets Field.

CHARLEY Baseball in this weather?

WILLY   Don't talk to him. Come on, come on! (*He is pushing them out.*)

CHARLEY Wait a minute, didn't you hear the news?

WILLY   What?

CHARLEY Don't you listen to the radio? Ebbets Field just blew up.

WILLY   You go to hell! (CHARLEY *laughs. Pushing them out.*) Come on, come on! We're late.

CHARLEY (*as they go*) Knock a homer, Biff, knock a homer!

WILLY   (*the last to leave, turning to* CHARLEY) I don't think that was funny, Charley. This is the greatest day of his life.

CHARLEY Willy, when are you going to grow up?

WILLY   Yeah, heh? When this game is over, Charley, you'll be laughing out of the other side of your face. They'll be calling him another Red Grange. Twenty-five thousand a year.

CHARLEY (*kidding*) Is that so?

WILLY   Yeah, that's so.

CHARLEY Well, then, I'm sorry, Willy. But tell me something.

WILLY What?

CHARLEY Who is Red Grange?

WILLY Put up your hands. Goddam you, put up your hands!

CHARLEY, chuckling, shakes his head and walks away, around the left corner of the stage. WILLY *follows him. The music rises to a mocking frenzy.*

WILLY Who the hell do you think you are, better than everybody else? You don't know everything, you big, ignorant, stupid ... Put up your hands!

Light rises, on the right side of the forestage, on a small table in the reception room of CHARLEY'S *office. Traffic sounds are heard.* BERNARD, *now mature, sits whistling to himself. A pair of tennis rackets and an overnight bag are on the floor beside him.*

WILLY (*offstage*) What are you walking away for? Don't walk away! If you're going to say something say it to my face! I know you laugh at me behind my back. You'll laugh out of the other side of your goddam face after this game. Touchdown! Touchdown! Eighty thousand people! Touchdown! Right between the goal posts.

BERNARD is a quiet, earnest, but self-assured young man. WILLY'S *voice is coming from right upstage now.* BERNARD *lowers his feet off the table and listens.* JENNY, *his father's secretary, enters.*

JENNY (*distressed*) Say, Bernard, will you go out in the hall?

BERNARD What is that noise? Who is it?

JENNY Mr Loman. He just got off the elevator.

BERNARD (*getting up*) Who's he arguing with?

JENNY Nobody. There's nobody with him. I can't deal with him any more, and your father gets all upset everytime he comes. I've got a lot of typing to do, and your father's waiting to sign it. Will you see him?

WILLY (*entering*) Touchdown! Touch — (*He sees* JENNY.)

Jenny, Jenny, good to see you. How're ya? Workin'?
Or still honest?

JENNY   Fine. How've you been feeling?

WILLY   Not much any more, Jenny. Ha, ha! (*He is surprised
to see the rackets.*)

BERNARD   Hello, Uncle Willy.

WILLY   (*almost shocked*) Bernard! Well, look who's here! *He
comes quickly, guiltily, to* BERNARD *and warmly
shakes his hand.*

BERNARD   How are you? Good to see you.

WILLY   What are you doing here?

BERNARD   Oh, just stopped by to see Pop. Get off my feet till
my train leaves. I'm going to Washington in a few
minutes.

WILLY   Is he in?

BERNARD   Yes, he's in his office with the accountant. Sit down.

WILLY   (*sitting down*) What're you going to do in
Washington?

BERNARD   Oh, just a case I've got there, Willy.

WILLY   That so? (*Indicating the rackets.*) You going to play
tennis there?

BERNARD   I'm staying with a friend who's got a court.

WILLY   Don't say. His own tennis court. Must be fine
people, I bet.

BERNARD   They are, very nice. Dad tells me Biff's in town.

WILLY   (*with a big smile*) Yeah, Biff's in. Working on a very
big deal, Bernard.

BERNARD   What's Biff doing?

WILLY   Well, he's been doing very big things in the West.
But he decided to establish himself here. Very big.
We're having dinner. Did I hear your wife had a
boy?

BERNARD   That's right. Our second.

WILLY   Two boys! What do you know!

BERNARD   What kind of a deal has Biff got?

WILLY	Well, Bill Oliver – very big sporting-goods man – he wants Biff very badly. Called him in from the West. Long distance, *carte blanche*, special deliveries. Your friends have their own private tennis court?
BERNARD	You still with the old firm, Willy?
WILLY	(*after a pause*) I'm – I'm overjoyed to see how you made the grade, Bernard, overjoyed. It's an encouraging thing to see a young man really – really – Looks very good for Biff – very – (*He breaks off, then.*) Bernard – (*He is so full of emotion, he breaks off again.*)
BERNARD	What is it, Willy?
WILLY	(*small and alone*) What – what's the secret?
BERNARD	What secret?
WILLY	How – how did you? Why didn't he ever catch on?
BERNARD	I wouldn't know that, Willy.
WILLY	(*confidentially, desperately*) You were his friend, his boyhood friend. There's something I don't understand about it. His life ended after that Ebbets Field game. From the age of seventeen nothing good ever happened to him.
BERNARD	He never trained himself for anything.
WILLY	But he did, he did. After high school he took so many correspondence courses. Radio mechanics; television; God knows what, and never made the slightest mark.
BERNARD	(*taking off his glasses*) Willy, do you want to talk candidly?
WILLY	(*rising, faces* BERNARD) I regard you as a very brilliant man, Bernard. I value your advice.
BERNARD	Oh, the hell with the advice, Willy. I couldn't advise you. There's just one thing I've always wanted to ask you. When he was supposed to graduate, and the math teacher flunked him —
WILLY	Oh, that son-of-a-bitch ruined his life.
BERNARD	Yeah, but, Willy, all he had to do was to go to summer school and make up that subject.
WILLY	That's right, that's right.

BERNARD Did you tell him not to go to summer school?

WILLY Me? I begged him to go. I ordered him to go!

BERNARD Then why wouldn't he go?

WILLY Why? Why? Bernard, that question has been trailing me like a ghost for the last fifteen years. He flunked the subject, and laid down and died like a hammer hit him!

BERNARD Take it easy, kid.

WILLY Let me talk to you – I got nobody to talk to. Bernard, Bernard, was it my fault? Y'see? It keeps going around in my mind, maybe I did something to him. I got nothing to give him.

BERNARD Don't take it so hard.

WILLY Why did he lay down? What is the story there? You were his friend!

BERNARD Willy, I remember, it was June, and our grades came out. And he'd flunked math.

WILLY That son-of-a-bitch!

BEN No, it wasn't right then. Biff just got very angry, I remember, and he was ready to enrol in summer school.

WILLY (*surprised*) He was?

BERNARD He wasn't beaten by it at all. But then, Willy, he disappeared from the block for almost a month. And I got the idea that he'd gone up to New England to see you. Did he have a talk with you then?

WILLY *stares in silence.*

BERNARD Willy?

WILLY (*with a strong edge of resentment in his voice*) Yeah, he came to Boston. What about it?

BERNARD Well, just that when he came back – I'll never forget this, it always mystifies me. Because I'd thought so well of Biff, even though he'd always taken advantage of me. I loved him, Willy, y'know? And he came back after that month and took his sneakers – remember those sneakers with 'University of Virginia' printed on them? He was so proud of those, wore them every day. And he took them down in the cellar, and burned them up in the furnace. We had a fist fight. It lasted at least half an hour. Just the two of us, punching each other down in the cellar, and crying right through it. I've often thought of how strange it was that I knew he'd given up his life. What happened in Boston, Willy?

WILLY *looks at him as at an intruder.*

BERNARD I just bring it up because you asked me.

WILLY (*angrily*) Nothing. What do you mean, 'What happened?' What's that got to do with anything?

BERNARD Well, don't get sore.

WILLY What are you trying to do, blame it on me? If a boy lays down is that my fault?

BERNARD Now, Willy, don't get —

WILLY Well, don't – don't talk to me that way! What does that mean, 'What happened?'

CHARLEY *enters. He is in his vest, and he carries a bottle of bourbon.*

CHARLEY Hey, you're going to miss that train. (*He waves the bottle.*)

BERNARD Yeah, I'm going. (*He takes the bottle.*) Thanks, Pop. (*He picks up his rackets and bag.*) Good-bye, Willy, and don't worry about it. You know, 'If at first you don't succeed ...'

WILLY Yes, I believe in that.

BERNARD But sometimes, Willy, it's better for a man just to walk away.

WILLY Walk away?

BERNARD That's right.

WILLY But if you can't walk away?

BERNARD (*after a slight pause*) I guess that's when it's tough. (*extending his hand*) Good-bye, Willy.

WILLY (*shaking* BERNARD'S *hand*) Good-bye, boy.

CHARLEY (*an arm on* BERNARD'S *shoulder*) How do you like this kid? Gonna argue a case in front of the Supreme Court.

BERNARD	(*protesting*) Pop!
WILLY	(*genuinely shocked, pained, and happy*) No! The Supreme Court!
BERNARD	I gotta run. 'Bye, Dad!
CHARLEY	Knock 'em dead, Bernard!

BERNARD *goes off.*

WILLY	(*as* CHARLEY *takes out his wallet*) The Supreme Court! And he didn't even mention it!
CHARLEY	(*counting out money on the desk*) He don't have to – he's gonna do it.
WILLY	And you never told him what to do, did you? You never took any interest in him.
CHARLEY	My salvation is that I never took any interest in anything. There's some money – fifty dollars. I got an accountant inside.
WILLY	Charley, look ... (*with difficulty*) I got my insurance to pay. If you can manage it – I need a hundred and ten dollars.

CHARLEY *doesn't reply for a moment, merely stops moving.*

WILLY	I'd draw it from my bank but Linda would know, and I ...
CHARLEY	Sit down, Willy.
WILLY	(*moving toward the chair*) I'm keeping an account of everything, remember. I'll pay every penny back. (*He sits.*)
CHARLEY	Now listen to me, Willy.
WILLY	I want you to know I appreciate ...
CHARLEY	(*sitting down on the table*) Willy, what're you doin'? What the hell is goin' on in your head?
WILLY	Why? I'm simply ...
CHARLEY	I offered you a job. You can make fifty dollars a week. And I won't send you on the road.
WILLY	I've got a job.
CHARLEY	Without pay? What kind of a job is a job without pay? (*He rises.*) Now, look, kid, enough is enough. I'm no genius but I know when I'm being insulted.

WILLY   Insulted!

CHARLEY   Why don't you want to work for me?

WILLY   What's the matter with you? I've got a job.

CHARLEY   Then what're you walkin' in here every week for?

WILLY   (*getting up*) Well, if you don't want me to walk in here —

CHARLEY   I am offering you a job.

WILLY   I don't want your goddam job!

CHARLEY   When the hell are you going to grow up?

WILLY   (*furiously*) You big ignoramus, if you say that to me again I'll rap you one! I don't care how big you are! (*He's ready to fight.*)

    Pause.

CHARLEY   (*kindly, going to him*) How much do you need, Willy?

WILLY   Charley, I'm strapped, I'm strapped. I don't know what to do. I was just fired.

CHARLEY   Howard fired you?

WILLY   That snotnose. Imagine that? I named him. I named him Howard.

CHARLEY   Willy, when're you gonna realize that them things don't mean anything? You named him Howard, but you can't sell that. The only thing you got in this world is what you can sell. And the funny thing is that you're a salesman, and you don't know that.

WILLY   I've always tried to think otherwise, I guess. I always felt that if a man was impressive, and well liked, that nothing —

CHARLEY   Why must everybody like you? Who liked J. P. Morgan? Was he impressive? In a Turkish bath he'd look like a butcher. But with his pockets on he was very well liked. Now listen, Willy, I know you don't like me, and nobody can say I'm in love with you, but I'll give you a job because – just for the hell of it, put it that way. Now what do you say?

WILLY I – I just can't work for you, Charley.

CHARLEY What're you, jealous of me?

WILLY I can't work for you, that's all, don't ask me why.

CHARLEY (*angered, takes out more bills*) You been jealous of me all your life, you damned fool! Here, pay your insurance. (*He puts the money in* WILLY'S *hand.*)

WILLY I'm keeping strict accounts.

CHARLEY I've got some work to do. Take care of yourself. And pay your insurance.

WILLY (*moving to the right*) Funny, y'know? After all the highways, and the trains, and the appointments, and the years, you end up worth more dead than alive.

CHARLEY Willy, nobody's worth nothin' dead. (*after a slight pause*) Did you hear what I said?

WILLY *stands still, dreaming.*

CHARLEY Willy!

WILLY Apologize to Bernard for me when you see him. I didn't mean to argue with him. He's a fine boy. They're all fine boys, and they'll end up big – all of them. Someday they'll all play tennis together. Wish me luck, Charley. He saw Bill Oliver today.

CHARLEY Good luck.

WILLY (*on the verge of tears*) Charley, you're the only friend I got. Isn't that a remarkable thing? (*He goes out.*)

CHARLEY Jesus!

CHARLEY *stares after him a moment and follows. All light blacks out. Suddenly raucous music is heard, and a red glow rises behind the screen at right.* STANLEY, *a young waiter, appears, carrying a table, followed by* HAPPY, *who is carrying two chairs.*

STANLEY (*putting the table down*) That's all right, Mr Loman, I can handle it myself. (*He turns and takes the chairs from* HAPPY *and places them at the table*).

HAPPY (*glancing around*) Oh, this is better.

STANLEY Sure, in the front there you're in the middle of all kinds of noise. Whenever you got a party, Mr Loman, you just tell me and I'll put you back here. Y'know, there's a lotta people they don't like in private, because when they go out they like to see a lotta action around them because they're sick and tired to stay in the house by theirself. But I know you, you ain't from Hackensack. You know what I mean?

HAPPY (*sitting down*) So how's it coming, Stanley?

STANLEY Ah, it's a dog's life. I only wish during the war they'd a took me in the Army. I coulda been dead by now.

HAPPY My brother's back, Stanley.

STANLEY Oh, he come back, heh? From the Far West.

HAPPY Yeah, big cattle man, my brother, so treat him right. And my father's coming too.

STANLEY Oh, your father too!

HAPPY You got a couple of nice lobsters?

STANLEY Hundred per cent, big.

HAPPY I want them with the claws.

STANLEY Don't worry, I don't give you no mice. (HAPPY *laughs*.) How about some wine? It'll put a head on the meal.

HAPPY No. You remember, Stanley, that recipe I brought you from overseas? With the champagne in it?

STANLEY Oh, yeah, sure. I still got it tacked up yet in the kitchen. But that'll have to cost a buck apiece anyways.

HAPPY That's all right.

STANLEY What'd you, hit a number or somethin'?

HAPPY No, it's a little celebration. My brother is – I think he pulled off a big deal today. I think we're going into business together.

STANLEY Great! That's the best for you. Because a family business, you know what I mean? – that's the best.

HAPPY That's what I think.

STANLEY 'Cause what's the difference? Somebody steals? It's in the family. Know what I mean? (*sotto voce*) Like this bartender here. The boss is goin' crazy what kinda leak he's got in the cash register. You put it in but it don't come out.

HAPPY (*raising his head*) Sh!

STANLEY What?

HAPPY You notice I wasn't lookin' right or left, was I?

STANLEY No.

HAPPY And my eyes are closed.

STANLEY So what's the —?

HAPPY Strudel's comin'.

STANLEY (*catching on, looks around*) Ah, no, there's no —
He breaks off as a furred, lavishly dressed girl enters and sits at the next table. Both follow her with their eyes.

STANLEY Geez, how'd ya know?

HAPPY I got radar or something. (*Staring directly at her profile.*) Oooooooo ... Stanley.

STANLEY I think that's for you, Mr Loman.

HAPPY Look at that mouth. Oh, God. And the binoculars.

STANLEY Geez, you got a life, Mr Loman.

HAPPY Wait on her.

STANLEY (*going to the girl's table*) Would you like a menu, ma'am?

GIRL I'm expecting someone, but I'd like a —

HAPPY Why don't you bring her – excuse me, miss, do you mind? I sell champagne, and I'd like you to try my brand. Bring her a champagne, Stanley.

GIRL That's awfully nice of you.

HAPPY Don't mention it. It's all company money. (*He laughs.*)

GIRL That's a charming product to be selling, isn't it?

HAPPY Oh, gets to be like everything else. Selling is selling, y'know.

GIRL I suppose.

HAPPY You don't happen to sell, do you?

GIRL No, I don't sell.

HAPPY Would you object to a compliment from a stranger? You ought to be on a magazine cover.

GIRL (*looking at him a little archly*) I have been.

STANLEY *comes in with a glass of champagne.*

HAPPY What'd I say before, Stanley? You see? She's a cover girl.

STANLEY Oh, I could see, I could see.

HAPPY (*to the* GIRL) What magazine?

GIRL Oh, a lot of them. (*She takes the drink.*) Thank you.

HAPPY You know what they say in France, don't you? 'Champagne is the drink of the complexion' – Hya, Biff!

BIFF *has entered and sits with* HAPPY.

BIFF Hello, kid. Sorry I'm late.

HAPPY I just got here. Uh, Miss —?

GIRL Forsythe.

HAPPY Miss Forsythe, this is my brother.

BIFF Is Dad here?

HAPPY His name is Biff. You might've heard of him. Great football player.

GIRL Really? What team?

HAPPY Are you familiar with football?

GIRL No, I'm afraid I'm not.

HAPPY Biff is a quarterback with the New York Giants.

GIRL Well, that is nice, isn't it? (*She drinks.*)

HAPPY Good health.

GIRL I'm happy to meet you.

HAPPY That's my name. Hap. It's really Harold, but at West Point they called me Happy.

GIRL (*now really impressed*) Oh, I see. How do you do? (*She turns her profile.*)

BIFF Isn't Dad coming?

HAPPY You want her?

BIFF Oh, I could never make that.

HAPPY I remember the time that idea would never come into your head. Where's the old confidence, Biff?

BIFF I just saw Oliver —

HAPPY Wait a minute. I've got to see that old confidence again. Do you want her? She's on call.

BIFF Oh, no. (*He turns to look at the* GIRL.)

HAPPY I'm telling you. Watch this. (*Turning to the* GIRL.) Honey? (*She turns to him.*) Are you busy?

GIRL Well, I am ... but I could make a phone call.

HAPPY Do that, will you, honey? And see if you can get a friend. We'll be here for a while. Biff is one of the greatest football players in the country.

GIRL (*standing up*) Well, I'm certainly glad to meet you.

HAPPY Come back soon.

GIRL I'll try.

HAPPY Don't try, honey, try hard.

The GIRL *exits.* STANLEY *follows her, shaking his head in bewildered admiration.*

HAPPY Isn't that a shame now? A beautiful girl like that? That's why I can't get married. There's not a good woman in a thousand. New York is loaded with them, kid!

BIFF Hap, look —

HAPPY I told you she was on call!

BIFF (*strangely unnerved*) Cut it out, will ya? I want to say something to you.

HAPPY Did you see Oliver?

BIFF I saw him all right. Now look, I want to tell Dad a couple of things and I want you to help me.

HAPPY What? Is he going to back you?

BIFF Are you crazy! You're out of your goddam head, you know that?

HAPPY Why? What happened?

BIFF (*breathlessly*) I did a terrible thing today, Hap. It's been the strangest day I ever went through. I'm all numb, I swear.

HAPPY You mean he wouldn't see you?

BIFF Well, I waited six hours for him, see? All day. Kept sending my name in. Even tried to date his secretary so she'd get me to him, but no soap.

HAPPY Because you're not shown' the old confidence, Biff. He remembered you, didn't he?

BIFF (*stopping* HAPPY *with a gesture*) Finally, about five o'clock, he comes out. Didn't remember who I was or anything. I felt like such an idiot, Hap.

HAPPY Did you tell him my Florida idea?

BIFF He walked away. I saw him for one minute. I got so mad I could've torn the walls down! How the hell did I ever get the idea I was a salesman there? I even believed myself that I'd been a salesman for him! And then he gave me one look and – I realized what a ridiculous lie my whole life has been. We've been talking in a dream for fifteen years. I was a shipping clerk.

HAPPY What'd you do?

BIFF (*with great tension and wonder*) Well, he left, see. And the secretary went out. I was all alone in the waiting-room. I don't know what came over me, Hap. The next thing I know I'm in his office – panelled walls, everything. I can't explain it. I – Hap, I took his fountain pen.

HAPPY Geez, did he catch you?

BIFF I ran out. I ran down all eleven flights. I ran and ran and ran.

HAPPY That was an awful dumb – what'd you do that for?

BIFF (*agonized*) I don't know, I just – wanted to take something, I don't know. You gotta help me, Hap, I'm gonna tell Pop.

HAPPY You crazy? What for?

BIFF Hap, he's got to understand that I'm not the man somebody lends that kind of money to. He thinks I've been spiting him all these years and it's eating him up.

HAPPY That's just it. You tell him something nice.

BIFF I can't.

HAPPY Say you got a lunch date with Oliver tomorrow.

BIFF So what do I do tomorrow?

HAPPY   You leave the house tomorrow and come back at
             night and say Oliver is thinking it over. And he
             thinks it over for a couple of weeks, and gradually it
             fades away and nobody's the worse.

BIFF   But it'll go on for ever!

HAPPY   Dad is never so happy as when he's looking
             forward to something!

             WILLY *enters.*

HAPPY   Hello, scout!

WILLY   Gee, I haven't been here in years!

             STANLEY *has followed* WILLY *in and sets a chair for*
             him. STANLEY *starts off but* HAPPY *stops him.*

HAPPY   Stanley!

             STANLEY *stands by, waiting for an order.*

BIFF   (*going to* WILLY *with guilt, as to an invalid*) Sit down,
             Pop. You want a drink?

WILLY   Sure, I don't mind.

BIFF   Let's get a load on.

WILLY   You look worried.

BIFF   N-no. (*To* STANLEY.) Scotch all around. Make it
             doubles.

STANLEY Doubles, right. (*He goes.*)

WILLY   You had a couple already, didn't you?

BIFF   Just a couple, yeah.

WILLY   Well, what happened, boy? (*Nodding affirmatively,*
             with a smile.) Everything go all right?

BIFF   (*takes a breath, then reaches out and grasps* WILLY'S
             hand) Pal ... (*He is smiling bravely, and* WILLY *is*
             smiling too.) I had an experience today.

HAPPY   Terrific, Pop.

WILLY   That so? What happened?

BIFF   (*high, slightly alcoholic, above the earth*) I'm going
             to tell you everything from first to last. It's been a
             strange day. (*Silence. He looks around, composes*
             himself as best he can, but his breath keeps breaking
             the rhythm of his voice.) I had to wait quite a while
             for him, and —

WILLY   Oliver?

BIFF   Yeah, Oliver. All day, as a matter of cold fact. And a lot of – instances – facts, Pop, facts about my life came back to me. Who was it, Pop? Who ever said I was a salesman with Oliver?

WILLY   Well, you were.

BIFF   No, Dad, I was a shipping clerk.

WILLY   But you were practically —

BIFF   (*with determination*) Dad, I don't know who said it first, but I was never a salesman for Bill Oliver.

WILLY   What're you talking about?

BIFF   Let's hold on to the facts tonight, Pop. We're not going to get anywhere bullin' around. I was a shipping clerk.

WILLY   (*angrily*) All right, now listen to me —

BIFF   Why don't you let me finish?

WILLY   I'm not interested in stories about the past or any crap of that kind because the woods are burning, boys, you understand? There's a big blaze going on all around. I was fired today.

BIFF   (*shocked*) How could you be?

WILLY   I was fired, and I'm looking for a little good news to tell your mother, because the woman has waited and the woman has suffered. The gist of it is that I haven't got a story left in my head, Biff. So don't give me a lecture about facts and aspects. I am not interested. Now what've you got to say to me?
STANLEY *enters with three drinks. They wait until he leaves.*

WILLY   Did you see Oliver?

BIFF   Jesus, Dad!

WILLY   You mean you didn't go up there?

HAPPY   Sure he went up there.

BIFF   I did. I – saw him. How could they fire you?

WILLY   (*on the edge of his chair*) What kind of a welcome did he give you?

BIFF   He won't even let you work on commission?

WILLY	I'm out! (*driving*) So tell me, he gave you a warm welcome?
HAPPY	Sure, Pop, sure!
BIFF	(*driven*) Well, it was kind of —
WILLY	I was wondering if he'd remember you. (*to* HAPPY) Imagine, man doesn't see him for ten, twelve years and gives him that kind of welcome!
HAPPY	Damn right!
BIFF	(*trying to return to the offensive*) Pop, look —
WILLY	You know why he remembered you, don't you? Because you impressed him in those days.
BIFF	Let's talk quietly and get this down to the facts, huh?
WILLY	(*as though* BIFF *had been interrupting*) Well, what happened? It's great news, Biff. Did he take you into his office or'd you talk in the waiting-room?
BIFF	Well, he came in, see, and —
WILLY	(*with a big smile*) What'd he say? Betcha he threw his arm around you.
BIFF	Well, he kinda —
WILLY	He's a fine man. (*to* HAPPY) Very hard man to see, y'know.
HAPPY	(*agreeing*) Oh, I know.
WILLY	(*to* BIFF) Is that where you had the drinks?
BIFF	Yeah, he gave me a couple of – no, no!
HAPPY	(*cutting in*) He told him my Florida idea.
WILLY	Don't interrupt. (*to* BIFF) How'd he react to the Florida idea?
BIFF	Dad, will you give me a minute to explain?
WILLY	I've been waiting for you to explain since I sat down here! What happened? He took you into his office and what?
BIFF	Well – I talked. And – and he listened, see.
WILLY	Famous for the way he listens, y'know. What was his answer?

BIFF His answer was — (*He breaks off, suddenly angry.*) Dad, you're not letting me tell you what I want to tell you!

WILLY (*accusing, angered*) You didn't see him, did you?

BIFF I did see him!

WILLY What'd you insult him or something? You insulted him, didn't you?

BIFF Listen, will you let me out of it, will you just let me out of it!

HAPPY What the hell!

WILLY Tell me what happened!

BIFF (*to* HAPPY) I can't talk to him!

A single trumpet note jars the air. The light of green leaves stains the house, which holds the air of night and a dream. YOUNG BERNARD *enters and knocks on the door of the house.*

YOUNG BERNARD (*frantically*) Mrs Loman, Mrs Loman!

HAPPY Tell him what happened!

BIFF (*to* HAPPY) Shut up and leave me alone!

WILLY No, no! You had to go and flunk math!

BIFF What math? What're you talking about?

YOUNG BERNARD Mrs Loman, Mrs Loman!

LINDA *appears in the house, as of old.*

WILLY (*wildly*) Math, math, math!

BIFF Take it easy, Pop!

YOUNG BERNARD Mrs Loman!

WILLY (*furiously*) If you hadn't flunked you'd've been set by now!

BIFF Now, look, I'm gonna tell you what happened, and you're going to listen to me.

YOUNG BERNARD Mrs Loman!

BIFF I waited six hours —

HAPPY What the hell are you saying?

BIFF I kept sending in my name but he wouldn't see me. So finally he ... (*He continues unheard as light fades low on the restaurant.*)

YOUNG BERNARD Biff flunked math!

LINDA No!

YOUNG BERNARD Birnbaum flunked him! They won't graduate him!

LINDA But they have to. He's gotta go to the university. Where is he? Biff? Biff?

YOUNG BERNARD No, he left. He went to Grand Central.

LINDA Grand – You mean he went to Boston!

YOUNG BERNARD Is Uncle Willy in Boston?

LINDA Oh, maybe Willy can talk to the teacher. Oh, the poor, poor boy!

Light on house area snaps out.

BIFF (*at the table, now audible, holding up a gold fountain pen*) ... so I'm washed up with Oliver, you understand? Are you listening to me?

WILLY (*at a loss*) Yeah, sure. If you hadn't flunked —

BIFF Flunked what? What're you talking about?

WILLY Don't blame everything on me! I didn't flunk math – you did! What pen?

HAPPY That was awful dumb, Biff, a pen like that is worth —

WILLY (*seeing the pen for the first time*) You took Oliver's pen?

BIFF (*weakening*) Dad, I just explained it to you.

WILLY You stole Bill Oliver's fountain pen!

BIFF I didn't exactly steal it! That's just what I've been explaining to you!

HAPPY He had it in his hand and just then Oliver walked in, so he got nervous and stuck it in his pocket!

WILLY My God, Biff!

BIFF I never intended to do it, Dad!

OPERATOR'S VOICE Standish Arms, good evening!

WILLY (*shouting*) I'm not in my room!

BIFF (*frightened*) Dad, what's the matter? (*He and* HAPPY *stand up.*)

OPERATOR Ringing Mr Loman for you!

WILLY I'm not there, stop it!

BIFF (*horrified, gets down on one knee before* WILLY) Dad, I'll make good, I'll make good. (WILLY *tries to get to his feet.* BIFF *holds him down.*) Sit down now.

WILLY No, you're no good. You're no good for anything.

BIFF I am, Dad, I'll find something else, you understand? Now don't worry about anything. (*He holds up* WILLY'S *face.*) Talk to me, Dad.

OPERATOR Mr Loman does not answer. Shall I page him?

WILLY (*attempting to stand, as though to rush and silence the* OPERATOR) No, no, no!

HAPPY He'll strike something, Pop.

WILLY No, no ...

BIFF (*desperately standing over* WILLY) Pop, listen! Listen to me! I'm telling you something good. Oliver talked to his partner about the Florida idea. You listening? He – he talked to his partner, and he came to me ... I'm going to be all right, you hear? Dad, listen to me, he said it was just a question of the amount!

WILLY Then you ... got it?

HAPPY He's gonna be terrific, Pop!

WILLY (*trying to stand*) Then you got it, haven't you? You got it! You got it!

BIFF (*agonized, holds* WILLY *down*) No, no. Look, Pop. I'm supposed to have lunch with them tomorrow. I'm just telling you this so you'll know that I can still make an impression, Pop. And I'll make good somewhere, but I can't go tomorrow, see?

WILLY Why not? You simply —

BIFF But the pen, Pop!

WILLY You give it to him and tell him it was an oversight!

HAPPY Sure, have lunch tomorrow!

BIFF I can't say that —

WILLY You were doing a crossword puzzle and accidentally used his pen!

BIFF   Listen, kid, I took those balls years ago, now I walk in with his fountain pen? That clinches it, don't you see? I can't face him like that! I'll try elsewhere.

PAGE'S VOICE   Paging Mr Loman!

WILLY   Don't you want to be anything?

BIFF   Pop, how can I go back?

WILLY   You don't want to be anything, is that what's behind it?

BIFF   (*now angry at* WILLY *for not crediting his sympathy*) Don't take it that way! You think it was easy walking into that office after what I'd done to him? A team of horses couldn't have dragged me back to Bill Oliver!

WILLY   Then why'd you go?

BIFF   Why did I go? Why did I go? Look at you! Look at what's become of you!
Off left, the WOMAN *laughs.*

WILLY   Biff, you're going to go to that lunch tomorrow, or —

BIFF   I can't go. I've got no appointment!

HAPPY   Biff, for ... !

WILLY   Are you spiting me?

BIFF   Don't take it that way! Goddammit!

WILLY   (*strikes* BIFF *and falters away from the table*) You rotten little louse! Are you spiting me?

THE WOMAN   Someone's at the door, Willy!

BIFF   I'm no good, can't you see what I am?

HAPPY   (*separating them*) Hey, you're in a restaurant! Now cut it out, both of you? (*The girls enter.*) Hello, girls, sit down.
The WOMAN *laughs, off left.*

MISS FORSYTHE   I guess we might as well. This is Letta.

THE WOMAN   Willy, are you going to wake up?

BIFF   (*ignoring* WILLY) How're ya, miss, sit down. What do you drink?

MISS FORSYTHE   Letta might not be able to stay long.

LETTA   I gotta get up very early tomorrow. I got jury duty. I'm so excited! Were you fellows ever on a jury?

BIFF   No, but I been in front of them! (*The girls laugh.*) This is my father.

LETTA   Isn't he cute? Sit down with us, Pop.

HAPPY   Sit him down, Biff!

BIFF   (*going to him*) Come on, slugger, drink us under the table. To hell with it! Come on, sit down, pal.

On BIFF'S *last insistence,* WILLY *is about to sit.*

THE WOMAN   (*now urgently*) Willy, are you going to answer the door!

The WOMAN'S *call pulls* WILLY *back. He starts right, befuddled.*

BIFF   Hey, where are you going?

WILLY   Open the door.

BIFF   The door?

WILLY   The washroom ... the door ... where's the door?

BIFF   (*leading* WILLY *to the left*) Just go straight down.

WILLY *moves left.*

THE WOMAN   Willy, Willy, are you going to get up, get up, get up, get up?

WILLY *exits left.*

LETTA   I think it's sweet you bring your daddy along.

MISS FORSYTHE   Oh, he isn't really your father!

BIFF   (*at left, turning to her resentfully*) Miss Forsythe, you've just seen a prince walk by. A fine, troubled prince. A hard-working, unappreciated prince. A pal, you understand? A good companion. Always for his boys.

LETTA   That's so sweet.

HAPPY   Well, girls, what's the programme? We're wasting time. Come on, Biff. Gather round. Where would you like to go?

BIFF   Why don't you do something for him?

HAPPY   Me!

BIFF   Don't you give a damn for him, Hap?

HAPPY What're you talking about? I'm the one who —

BIFF I sense it, you don't give a good goddam about him. (*He takes the rolled-up hose from his pocket and puts it on the table in front of* HAPPY.) Look what I found in the cellar, for Christ's sake. How can you bear to let it go on?

HAPPY Me? Who goes away? Who runs off and —

BIFF Yeah, but he doesn't mean anything to you. You could help him – I can't. Don't you understand what I'm talking about? He's going to kill himself, don't you know that?

HAPPY Don't I know it! Me!

BIFF Hap, help him! Jesus ... help him ... Help me, help me, I can't bear to look at his face! (*Ready to weep, he hurries out, up right.*)

HAPPY (*starting after him*) Where are you going?

MISS FORSYTHE What's he so mad about?

HAPPY Come on girls, we'll catch up with him.

MISS FORSYTHE (*as* HAPPY *pushes her out*) Say, I don't like that temper of his!

HAPPY He's just a little overstrung, he'll be all right!

WILLY (*off left, as the* WOMAN *laughs*) Don't answer! Don't answer!

LETTA Don't you want to tell your father —

HAPPY No, that's not my father. He's just a guy. Come on, we'll catch Biff, and, honey, we're going to paint this town! Stanley, where's the check! Hey, Stanley!

They exit. STANLEY *looks toward left.*

STANLEY (*calling to* HAPPY *indignantly*) Mr Loman! Mr Loman!

STANLEY *picks up a chair and follows them off. Knocking is heard off left. The* WOMAN *enters, laughing.* WILLY *follows her. She is in a black slip; he is buttoning his shirt. Raw, sensuous music accompanies their speech.*

WILLY Will you stop laughing? Will you stop?

THE WOMAN   Aren't you going to answer the door? He'll wake the whole hotel.

WILLY   I'm not expecting anybody.

THE WOMAN   Whyn't you have another drink, honey, and stop being so damn self-centred?

WILLY   I'm so lonely.

THE WOMAN   You know you ruined me, Willy? From now on, whenever you come to the office, I'll see that you go right through to the buyers. No waiting at my desk any more, Willy. You ruined me.

WILLY   That's nice of you to say that.

THE WOMAN   Gee, you are self-centred! Why so sad? You are the saddest, self-centredest soul I ever did see-saw. (*She laughs. He kisses her.*) Come on inside, drummer boy. It's silly to be dressing in the middle of the night. (*As knocking is heard.*) Aren't you going to ' answer the door?

WILLY   They're knocking on the wrong door.

THE WOMAN   But I felt the knocking. And he heard us talking in here. Maybe the hotel's on fire!

WILLY   (*his terror rising*) It's a mistake.

THE WOMAN   Then tell him to go away!

WILLY   There's nobody there.

THE WOMAN   It's getting on my nerves. Willy. There's somebody standing out there and it's getting on my nerves!

WILLY   (*pushing her away from him*) All right, stay in the bathroom here, and don't come out. I think there's a law in Massachusetts about it, so don't come out. It may be that new room clerk. He looked very mean. So don't come out. It's a mistake, there's no fire.

The knocking is heard again. He takes a few steps away from her, and she vanishes into the wing. The light follows him, and now he is facing YOUNG BIFF, *who carries a suitcase.* BIFF *steps toward him. The music is gone.*

BIFF   Why didn't you answer?

WILLY   Biff! What are you doing in Boston?

BIFF Why didn't you answer! I've been knocking for five minutes, I called you on the phone —

WILLY I just heard you. I was in the bathroom and had the door shut. Did anything happen home?

BIFF Dad – I let you down.

WILLY What do you mean?

BIFF Dad ...

WILLY Biffo, what's this about? (*Putting his arm around* BIFF.) Come on, let's go downstairs and get you a malted.

BIFF Dad, I flunked math.

WILLY Not for the term?

BIFF The term. I haven't got enough credits to graduate.

WILLY You mean to say Bernard wouldn't give you the answers?

BIFF He did, he tried, but I only got a sixty-one.

WILLY And they wouldn't give you four points?

BIFF Birnbaum refused absolutely. I begged him, Pop, but he won't give me those points. You gotta talk to him before they close the school. Because if he saw the kind of man you are, and you just talked to him in your way, I'm sure he'd come through for me. The class came right before practice, see, and I didn't go enough. Would you talk to him? He'd like you, Pop. You know the way you could talk.

WILLY You're on. We'll drive right back.

BIFF Oh, Dad, good work! I'm sure he'll change it for you!

WILLY Go downstairs and tell the clerk I'm checkin' out. Go right down.

BIFF Yes, sir! See, the reason he hates me, Pop – one day he was late for class so I got up at the blackboard and imitated him. I crossed my eyes and talked with a lithp.

WILLY (*laughing*) You did? The kids like it?

BIFF They nearly died laughing!

WILLY Yeah? What'd you do?

BIFF The thquare root of thixthy twee is ... (WILLY *bursts out* *laughing;* BIFF *joins him.*) And in the middle of it he walked in!

WILLY *laughs and the* WOMAN *joins in offstage.*

WILLY (*without hesitation*) Hurry downstairs and —

BIFF Somebody in there?

WILLY No, that was next door.

The WOMAN *laughs offstage.*

BIFF Somebody got in your bathroom!

WILLY No, it's the next room, there's a party —

THE WOMAN (*enters, laughing. She lisps this*) Can I come in? There's something in the bathtub, Willy, and it's moving! (WILLY *looks at* BIFF, *who is staring openmouthed and horrified at the* WOMAN.)

WILLY Ah – you better go back to your room. They must be finished painting by now. They're painting her room so I let her take a shower here. Go back, go back ... (*He pushes her.*)

THE WOMAN (*resisting*) But I've got to get dressed, Willy, I can't —

WILLY Get out of here! Go back, go back ... (*Suddenly striving for the ordinary.*) This is Miss Francis, Biff, she's a buyer. They're painting her room. Go back, Miss Francis, go back ...

THE WOMAN But my clothes, I can't go out naked in the hall!

WILLY (*pushing her offstage*) Get outa here! Go back, go back!

BIFF *slowly sits down on his suitcase as the argument continues offstage.*

THE WOMAN Where's my stockings? You promised me stockings, Willy!

WILLY I have no stockings here!

THE WOMAN You had two boxes of size nine sheers for me, and I want them!

WILLY Here, for God's sake, will you get outa here!

THE WOMAN (*enters holding a box of stockings*) I just hope there's nobody in the hall. That's all I hope. (*to* BIFF) Are you football or baseball?

BIFF Football.

THE WOMAN (*angry, humiliated*) That's me too. G'night. (*She snatches her clothes from* WILLY, *and walks out.*)

WILLY (*after a pause*) Well, better get going. I want to get to the school first thing in the morning. Get my suits out of the closet. I'll get my valise. (BIFF *doesn't move.*) What's the matter? (BIFF *remains motionless, tears falling.*) She's a buyer. Buys for J. H. Simmons. She lives down the hall – they're painting. You don't imagine — (*He breaks off. After a pause.*) Now listen, pal, she's just a buyer. She sees merchandise in her room and they have to keep it looking just so ... (*Pause. Assuming command.*) All right, get my suits. (BIFF *doesn't move.*) Now stop crying and do as I say. I gave you an order. Biff, I gave you an order! Is that what you do when I give you an order? How dare you cry? (*Putting his arm around* BIFF.) Now look, Biff, when you grow up you'll understand about these things. You mustn't – you mustn't over-emphasize a thing like this. I'll see Birnbaum first thing in the morning.

BIFF Never mind.

WILLY (*getting down beside* BIFF) Never mind! He's going to give you those points. I'll see to it.

BIFF He wouldn't listen to you.

WILLY He certainly will listen to me. You need those points for the U. of Virginia.

BIFF I'm not going there.

WILLY Heh? If I can't get him to change that mark you'll make it up in summer school. You've got all summer to —

BIFF (*his weeping breaking from him*) Dad ...

WILLY (*infected by it*) Oh, my boy ...

BIFF Dad ...

WILLY She's nothing to me, Biff. I was lonely, I was terribly lonely.

BIFF   You – you gave her Mama's stockings! (*His tears break through and he rises to go.*)

WILLY   (*grabbing for* BIFF) I gave you an order!

BIFF   Don't touch me, you – liar!

WILLY   Apologize for that!

BIFF   You fake! You phoney little fake! You fake! (*Overcome he turns quickly and weeping fully goes out with his suitcase.* WILLY *is left on the floor on his knees.*)

WILLY   I gave you an order! Biff, come back here or I'll beat you! Come back here! I'll whip you!

    STANLEY *comes quickly in from the right and stands in front of* WILLY.

WILLY   (*shouts at* STANLEY) I gave you an order ...

STANLEY   Hey, let's pick it up, pick it up, Mr Loman. (*He helps* WILLY *to his feet.*) Your boys left with the chippies. They said they'll see you home.

    A second waiter watches some distance away.

WILLY   But we were supposed to have dinner together.

    Music is heard, WILLY'S *theme.*

STANLEY   Can you make it?

WILLY   I'll – sure, I can make it. (*Suddenly concerned about his clothes.*) Do I – I look all right?

STANLEY   Sure, you look all right. (*He flicks a speck off* WILLY'S *lapel.*)

WILLY   Here – here's a dollar.

STANLEY   Oh, your son paid me. It's all right.

WILLY   (*putting it in* STANLEY'S *hand*) No, take it. You're a good boy.

STANLEY   Oh, no, you don't have to ...

WILLY   Here – here's some more. I don't need it any more. (*After a slight pause.*) Tell me – is there a seed store in the neighbourhood?

STANLEY   Seeds? You mean like to plant?

    As WILLY *turns,* STANLEY *slips the money back into his jacket pocket.*

WILLY   Yes. Carrots, peas ...

STANLEY   Well, there's hardware stores on Sixth Avenue, but it may be too late now.

WILLY   (*anxiously*) Oh, I'd better hurry. I've got to get some seeds. (*He starts off to the right.*) I've got to get some seeds, right away. Nothing's planted. I don't have a thing in the ground.

WILLY hurries out as the light goes down. STANLEY moves over to the right after him, watches him off. The other waiter has been staring at WILLY.

STANLEY   (*to the waiter*) Well, whatta you looking at?

The waiter picks up the chairs and moves off right. STANLEY takes the table and follows him. The light fades on this area. There is a long pause, the sound of the flute coming over. The light gradually rises on the kitchen, which is empty. HAPPY appears at the door of the house, followed by BIFF. HAPPY is carrying a large bunch of long-stemmed roses. He enters the kitchen, looks around for LINDA. Not seeing her, he turns to BIFF, who is just outside the house door, and makes a gesture with his hands, indicating 'Not here, I guess'. He looks into the living-room and freezes. Inside, LINDA, unseen, is seated, WILLY's coat on her lap. She rises ominously and quietly and moves toward HAPPY, who backs up into the kitchen, afraid.

HAPPY   Hey, what're you doing up? (LINDA *says nothing but moves toward him implacably.*) Where's Pop? (*He keeps backing to the right, and now* LINDA *is in full view in the doorway to the living-room.*) Is he sleeping?

LINDA   Where were you?

HAPPY   (*trying to laugh it off*) We met two girls, Mom, very fine types. Here, we brought you some flowers. (*Offering them to her.*) Put them in your room, Ma. *She knocks them to the floor at* BIFF's *feet. He has now come inside and closed the door behind him. She stares at* BIFF, *silent.*

HAPPY   Now what'd you do that for? Mom, I want you to
             have some flowers —

LINDA   (*cutting* HAPPY *off, violently to* BIFF) Don't you care
             whether he lives or dies?

HAPPY   (*going to the stairs*) Come upstairs, Biff.

BIFF   (*with a flare of disgust, to* HAPPY) Go away from me!
             (*To* LINDA.) What do you mean, lives or dies?
             Nobody's dying around here, pal.

LINDA   Get out of my sight! Get out of here!

BIFF   I wanna see the boss.

LINDA   You're not going near him!

BIFF   Where is he? (*He moves into the living-room and*
             LINDA *follows.*)

LINDA   (*shouting after* BIFF) You invite him to dinner. He
             looks forward to it all day — (BIFF *appears in his*
             parents' bedroom, looks around, and exits) – and
             then you desert him there. There's no stranger you'd
             do that to!

HAPPY   Why? He had a swell time with us. Listen, when I –
             (LINDA *comes back into the kitchen*) – desert him I
             hope I don't outlive the day!

LINDA   Get out of here!

HAPPY   Now look, Mom ...

LINDA   Did you have to go to women tonight? You and your
             lousy rotten whores!
             BIFF *re-enters the kitchen.*

HAPPY   Mom, all we did was follow Biff around trying to
             cheer him up! (*to* BIFF) Boy, what a night you gave me!

LINDA   Get out of here, both of you, and don't come back!
             I don't want you tormenting him any more. Go on
             now, get your things together! (*to* BIFF) You can
             sleep in his apartment. (*She starts to pick up the*
             flowers and stops herself.) Pick up this stuff, I'm not
             your maid any more. Pick it up, you bum, you!
             HAPPY *turns his back to her in refusal.* BIFF *slowly*
             moves over and gets down on his knees, picking up
             the flowers.

LINDA You're a pair of animals! Not one, not another living soul would have had the cruelty to walk out on that man in a restaurant!

BIFF (*not looking at her*) Is that what he said?

LINDA He didn't have to say anything. He was so humiliated he nearly limped when he came in.

HAPPY But, Mom, he had a great time with us —

BIFF (*cutting him off violently*) – Shut up!

Without another word, HAPPY *goes upstairs.*

LINDA You! You didn't even go in to see if he was all right!

BIFF (*still on the floor in front of* LINDA, *the flowers in his hand; with self-loathing*) No. Didn't. Didn't do a damned thing. How do you like that, heh? Left him babbling in a toilet.

LINDA You louse. You ...

BIFF Now you hit it on the nose! (*He gets up, throws the flowers in the wastebasket.*) The scum of the earth, and you're looking at him!

LINDA Get out of here!

BIFF I gotta talk to the boss, Mom. Where is he?

LINDA You're not going near him. Get out of this house!

BIFF (*with absolute assurance, determination*) No. We're gonna have an abrupt conversation, him and me.

LINDA You're not talking to him!

Hammering is heard from outside the house, off right. BIFF *turns toward the noise.*

LINDA (*suddenly pleading*) Will you please leave him alone?

BIFF What's he doing out there?

LINDA He's planting the garden!

BIFF (*quietly*) Now? Oh, my God!

BIFF moves outside, LINDA *following. The light dies down on them and comes up on the centre of the apron as* WILLY *walks into it. He is carrying a flashlight, a hoe, and a handful of seed packets. He raps the top of the hoe sharply to fix it firmly, and then moves to the left, measuring off the distance*

with his foot. He holds the flashlight to look at the seed
packets, reading off the instructions. He is in the blue
of night.

WILLY Carrots ... quarter-inch apart. Rows ... one-foot rows.
(*He measures it off.*) One foot. (*He puts down a*
package and measures off.) Beets. (*He puts down*
another packet and measures again.) Lettuce. (*He*
reads the package, puts it down.) One foot – (*He*
breaks off as BEN *appears to the right and moves slowly*
down to him.) What a proposition, ts, ts. Terrific,
terrific. 'Cause she's suffered, Ben, the woman has
suffered. You understand me? A man can't go out the
way he came in, Ben, a man has got to add up to
something. You can't, you can't – (BEN *moves toward*
him as though to interrupt.) You gotta consider, now.
Don't answer so quick. Remember, it's a guaranteed
twenty-thousand-dollar proposition. Now look, Ben, I
want you to go through the ins and outs of this thing
with me. I've got nobody to talk to, Ben, and the
woman has suffered, you hear me?

BEN (*standing still, considering*) What's the proposition?

WILLY It's twenty thousand dollars on the barrelhead.
Guaranteed, gilt-edged, you understand?

BEN You don't want to make a fool of yourself. They
might not honour the policy.

WILLY How can they dare refuse? Didn't I work like a
coolie to meet every premium on the nose? And
now they don't pay off! Impossible!

BEN It's called a cowardly thing, William.

WILLY Why? Does it take more guts to stand here the rest of
my life ringing up a zero?

BEN (*yielding*) That's a point, William. (*He moves,*
thinking, turns.) And twenty thousand – that *is*
something one can feel with the hand, it is there.

WILLY (*now assured, with rising power*) Oh, Ben, that's
the whole beauty of it! I see it like a diamond,
shining in the dark, hard and rough, that I
can pick up and touch in my hand. Not like –
like an appointment! This would not be

another damned-fool appointment, Ben, and it
changes all the aspects. Because he thinks I'm
nothing, see, and so he spites me. But the funeral –
(*straightening up*) Ben, that funeral will be massive!
They'll come from Maine, Massachusetts, Vermont,
New Hampshire! All the old-timers with the strange
licence plates – that boy will be thunderstruck, Ben,
because he never realized – I am known! Rhode
Island, New York, New Jersey – I am known, Ben,
and he'll see it with his eyes once and for all. He'll
see what I am, Ben! He's in for a shock, that boy!

BEN   (*coming down to the edge of the garden*) He'll call
you a coward.

WILLY   (*suddenly fearful*) No, that would be terrible.

BEN   Yes. And a damned fool.

WILLY   No, no, he mustn't, I won't have that! (*He is broken
and desperate.*)

BEN   He'll hate you, William.
The gay music of the boys is heard.

WILLY   Oh, Ben, how do we get back to all the great times?
Used to be so full of light, and comradeship, the
sleigh-riding in winter, and the ruddiness on his
cheeks. And always some kind of good news coming
up, always something nice coming up ahead. And
never even let me carry the valises in the house, and
simonizing, simonizing that little red car! Why, why
can't I give him something and not have him hate
me?

BEN   Let me think about it. (*He glances at his watch.*) I still
have a little time. Remarkable proposition, but you've
got to be sure you're not making a fool of yourself.
BEN *drifts off upstage and goes out of sight.* BIFF *comes
down from the left.*

WILLY   (*suddenly conscious of* BIFF, *turns and looks up at him,
then begins picking up the packages of seeds in
confusion*) Where the hell is that seed? (*indignantly*)
You can't see nothing out here! They boxed in the
whole goddam neighbourhood!

BIFF   There are people all around here. Don't you realize that?

WILLY   I'm busy. Don't bother me.

BIFF   (*taking the hoe from* WILLY) I'm saying good-bye to you, Pop. (WILLY *looks at him, silent, unable to move.*) I'm not coming back any more.

WILLY   You're not going to see Oliver tomorrow?

BIFF   I've got no appointment, Dad.

WILLY   He put his arm around you, and you've got no appointment?

BIFF   Pop, get this now, will you? Every time I've left it's been a fight that sent me out of here. Today I realized something about myself and I tried to explain it to you and I – I think I'm just not smart enough to make any sense out of it for you. To hell with whose fault it is or anything like that. (*He takes* WILLY's *arm.*) Let's just wrap it up, heh? Come on in, we'll tell Mom. (*He gently tries to pull* WILLY *to left.*)

WILLY   (*frozen, immobile, with guilt in his voice*) No, I don't want to see her.

BIFF   Come on! (*He pulls again, and* WILLY *tries to pull away.*)

WILLY   (*highly nervous*) No, no, I don't want to see her.

BIFF   (*tries to look into* WILLY's *face, as if to find the answer there*) Why don't you want to see her?

WILLY   (*more harshly now*) Don't bother me, will you?

BIFF   What do you mean, you don't want to see her? You don't want them calling you yellow, do you? This isn't your fault; it's me, I'm a bum. Now come inside! (WILLY *strains to get away.*) Did you hear what I said to you?

WILLY *pulls away and quickly goes by himself into the house.* BIFF *follows.*

LINDA   (*to* WILLY) Did you plant, dear?

BIFF   (*at the door, to* LINDA) All right, we had it out. I'm going and I'm not writing any more.

LINDA   (*going to* WILLY *in the kitchen*) I think that's the best way, dear. 'Cause there's no use drawing it out, you'll just never get along.

WILLY *doesn't respond.*

BIFF People ask where I am and what I'm doing, you don't know, and you don't care. That way it'll be off your mind and you can start brightening up again. All right? That clears it, doesn't it? (WILLY *is silent, and* BIFF *goes to him.*) You gonna wish me luck, scout! (*He extends his hand.*) What do you say?

LINDA Shake his hand, Willy.

WILLY (*turning to her, seething with hurt*) There's no necessity to mention the pen at all, y'know.

BIFF (*gently*) I've got no appointment, Dad.

WILLY (*erupting fiercely*) He put his arm around ... ?

BIFF Dad, you're never going to see what I am, so what's the use of arguing? If I strike oil I'll send you a cheque. Meantime forget I'm alive.

WILLY (*to* LINDA) Spite, see?

BIFF Shake hands, Dad.

WILLY Not my hand.

BIFF I was hoping not to go this way.

WILLY Well, this is the way you're going. Good-bye.

BIFF *looks at him a moment, then turns sharply and goes to the stairs.*

WILLY (*stops him with*) May you rot in hell if you leave this house!

BIFF (*turning*) Exactly what is it that you want from me?

WILLY I want you to know, on the train, in the mountains, in the valleys, wherever you go, that you cut down your life for spite!

BIFF No, no.

WILLY Spite, spite, is the word of your undoing! And when you're down and out, remember what did it. When you're rotting somewhere beside the railroad tracks, remember, and don't you dare blame it on me!

BIFF   I'm not blaming it on you!

WILLY   I won't take the rap for this, you hear?

HAPPY *comes down the stairs and stands on the bottom step, watching.*

BIFF   That's just what I'm telling you!

WILLY   (*sinking into a chair at the table, with full accusation*) You're trying to put a knife in me – don't think I don't know what you're doing!

BIFF   All right, phoney! Then let's lay it on the line. (*He whips the rubber tube from his pocket and puts it on the table.*)

HAPPY   You crazy —

LINDA   Biff! (*She moves to grab the hose, but* BIFF *holds it down with his hand.*)

BIFF   Leave it there! Don't move it!

WILLY   (*not looking at it*) What is that?

BIFF   You know goddam well what that is.

WILLY   (*caged, wanting to escape*) I never saw that.

BIFF   You saw it. The mice didn't bring it into the cellar! What is this supposed to do, make a hero out of you? This supposed to make me sorry for you?

WILLY   Never heard of it.

BIFF   There'll be no pity for you, you hear it? No pity!

WILLY   (*to* LINDA) You heard the spite!

BIFF   No, you're going to hear the truth – what you are and what I am!

LINDA   Stop it!

WILLY   Spite!

HAPPY   (*coming down toward* BIFF) You cut it now!

BIFF   (*to* HAPPY) The man don't know who we are! The man is gonna know! (*to* WILLY) We never told the truth for ten minutes in this house!

HAPPY   We always told the truth!

BIFF   (*turning on him*) You big blow, are you the assistant buyer? You're one of the two assistants to the assistant, aren't you?

HAPPY Well, I'm practically —

BIFF You're practically full of it! We all are! And I'm through with it. (*to* WILLY) Now hear this, Willy, this is me.

WILLY I know you!

BIFF You know why I had no address for three months? I stole a suit in Kansas City and I was in jail. (*To* LINDA, *who is sobbing.*) Stop crying. I'm through with it.

LINDA *turns away from them, her hands covering her face.*

WILLY I suppose that's my fault!

BIFF I stole myself out of every good job since high school!

WILLY And whose fault is that?

BIFF And I never got anywhere because you blew me so full of hot air I could never stand taking orders from anybody! That's whose fault it is!

WILLY I hear that!

LINDA Don't, Biff!

BIFF It's goddam time you heard that! I had to be boss big shot in two weeks, and I'm through with it!

WILLY Then hang yourself! For spite, hang yourself!

BIFF No! Nobody's hanging himself, Willy! I ran down eleven flights with a pen in my hand today. And suddenly I stopped, you hear me? And in the middle of that office building, do you hear this? I stopped in the middle of that building and I saw – the sky. I saw the things that I love in this world. The work and the food and time to sit and smoke. And I looked at the pen and said to myself, what the hell am I grabbing this for? Why am I trying to become what I don't want to be? What am I doing in an office, making a contemptuous, begging fool of myself, when all I want is out there, waiting for me the minute I say I know who I am! Why can't I say that, Willy? (*He tries to make* WILLY *face him, but* WILLY *pulls away and moves to the left.*)

WILLY (*with hatred, threateningly*) The door of your life is wide open!

BIFF   Pop! I'm a dime a dozen, and so are you!

WILLY   (*turning on him now in an uncontrolled outburst*) I am not a dime a dozen! I am Willy Loman, and you are Biff Loman!

BIFF *starts for* WILLY, *but is blocked by* HAPPY. *In his fury,* BIFF *seems on the edge of attacking his father.*

BIFF   I am not a leader of men, Willy, and neither are you. You were never anything but a hard-working drummer who landed in the ash-can like all the rest of them! I'm one dollar an hour, Willy! I tried seven states and couldn't raise it. A buck an hour! Do you gather my meaning? I'm not bringing home any prizes any more, and you're going to stop waiting for me to bring them home!

WILLY   (*directly to* BIFF) You vengeful, spiteful mutt!

BIFF *breaks from* HAPPY. WILLY, *in fright, starts up the stairs.* BIFF *grabs him.*

BIFF   (*at the peak of his fury*) Pop, I'm nothing! I'm nothing, Pop. Can't you understand that? There's no spite in it any more. I'm just what I am, that's all.

BIFF'S *fury has spent itself, and he breaks down, sobbing, holding on to* WILLY, *who dumbly fumbles for* BIFF'S *face.*

WILLY   (*astonished*) What're you doing? What're you doing? (*to* LINDA) Why is he crying?

BIFF   (*crying, broken*) Will you let me go, for Christ's sake? Will you take that phoney dream and burn it before something happens? (*Struggling to contain himself, he pulls away and moves up the stairs.*) I'll go in the morning. Put him – put him to bed. (*Exhausted,* BIFF *moves up the stairs to his room.*)

WILLY   (*after a long pause, astonished, elevated*) Isn't that – isn't that remarkable? Biff – he likes me!

LINDA   He loves you, Willy!

HAPPY   (*deeply moved*) Always did, Pop.

WILLY   Oh, Biff! (*staring wildly*) He cried! Cried to me. (*He is choking with his love, and now cries out his promise.*) That boy – that boy is going to be magnificent!

BEN *appears in the light just outside the kitchen.*

BEN   Yes, outstanding, with twenty thousand behind him.

LINDA   (*sensing the racing of his mind, fearfully, carefully*) Now come to bed, Willy. It's all settled now.

WILLY   (*finding it difficult not to rush out of the house*) Yes, we'll sleep. Come on. Go to sleep, Hap.

BEN   And it does take a great kind of a man to crack the jungle.

In accents of dread, BEN'S *idyllic music starts up.*

HAPPY   (*his arm around* LINDA) I'm getting married, Pop, don't forget it. I'm changing everything. I'm gonna run that department before the year is up. You'll see, Mom. (*He kisses her.*)

BEN   The jungle is dark but full of diamonds, Willy.

WILLY *turns, moves, listening to* BEN.

LINDA   Be good. You're both good boys, just act that way, that's all.

HAPPY   'Night, Pop. (*He goes upstairs.*)

LINDA   (*to* WILLY) Come, dear.

BEN   (*with greater force*) One must go in to fetch a diamond out.

WILLY   (*to* LINDA, *as he moves slowly along the edge of the kitchen, toward the door*) I just want to get settled down, Linda. Let me sit alone for a little.

LINDA   (*almost uttering her fear*) I want you upstairs.

WILLY   (*taking her in his arms*) In a few minutes, Linda. I couldn't sleep right now. Go on, you look awful tired. (*He kisses her.*)

BEN   Not like an appointment at all. A diamond is rough and hard to the touch.

WILLY   Go on now. I'll be right up.

LINDA   I think this is the only way, Willy.

WILLY   Sure, it's the best thing.

BEN   Best thing!

WILLY   The only way. Everything is gonna be – go on, kid, get to bed. You look so tired.

LINDA   Come right up.

WILLY   Two minutes.

    LINDA *goes into the living-room, then reappears in her bedroom.* WILLY *moves just outside the kitchen door.*

WILLY   Loves me. (*wonderingly*) Always loved me. Isn't that a remarkable thing? Ben, he'll worship me for it!

BEN   (*with promise*) It's dark there, but full of diamonds.

WILLY   Can you imagine that magnificence with twenty thousand dollars in his pocket?

LINDA   (*calling from her room*) Willy! Come up!

WILLY   (*calling into the kitchen*) Yes! Yes. Coming! It's very smart, you realize that, don't you, sweetheart? Even Ben sees it. I gotta go, baby. 'Bye! 'Bye! (*Going over to* BEN, *almost dancing.*) Imagine? When the mail comes he'll be ahead of Bernard again!

BEN   A perfect proposition all round.

WILLY   Did you see how he cried to me? Oh, if I could kiss him, Ben!

BEN   Time, William, time!

WILLY   Oh, Ben, I always knew one way or another we were gonna make it, Biff and I!

BEN   (*looking at his watch*) The boat. We'll be late. (*He moves slowly off into the darkness.*)

WILLY   (*elegiacally, turning to the house*) Now when you kick off, boy, I want a seventy-yard boot, and get right down the field under the ball, and when you hit, hit low and hit hard, because it's important, boy. (*He swings round and faces the audience.*) There's all kinds of important people in the stands, and the first thing you know ... (*Suddenly realizing he is alone.*) Ben! Ben, where do I ... ? (*He makes a sudden movement of searching.*) Ben, how do I ... ?

LINDA   (*calling*) Willy, you coming up?

WILLY   (*uttering a gasp of fear, whirling about as if to quiet her*) Sh! (*He turns around as if to find his way; sounds, faces, voices, seem to be swarming in upon him and he flicks at them, crying,*

'Sh! Sh!' *Suddenly music, faint and high, stops him.*
It rises in intensity, almost to an unbearable scream.
He goes up and down on his toes, and rushes off
around the house.) Shhh!

LINDA Willy?

There is no answer. LINDA *waits.* BIFF *gets up off his*
bed. He is still in his clothes. HAPPY *sits up.* BIFF *stands*
listening.

LINDA (*with real fear*) Willy, answer me! Willy!

There is the sound of a car starting and moving
away at full speed.

LINDA No!

BIFF (*rushing down the stairs*) Pop!

As the car speeds off, the music crashes down in a
frenzy of sound, which becomes the soft pulsation of
a single 'cello string. BIFF *slowly returns to his*
bedroom. He and HAPPY *gravely don their jackets.*
LINDA *slowly walks out of her room. The music has*
developed into a dead march. The leaves of day are
appearing over everything. CHARLEY *and* BERNARD,
sombrely dressed, appear and knock on the kitchen
door. BIFF *and* HAPPY *slowly descend the stairs to the*
kitchen as CHARLEY *and* BERNARD *enter. All stop a*
moment when LINDA, *in clothes of mourning, bearing*
a little bunch of roses, comes through the draped
doorway into the kitchen. She goes to CHARLEY *and*
takes his arm. Now all move toward the audience,
through the wall-line of the kitchen. At the limit of
the apron, LINDA *lays down the flowers, kneels, and*
sits back on her heels. All stare down at the grave.

REQUIEM

CHARLEY   It's getting dark, Linda.

   LINDA *doesn't react. She stares at the grave.*

BIFF   How about it, Mom? Better get some rest, heh? They'll be closing the gate soon.

   LINDA *makes no move. Pause.*

HAPPY   (*deeply angered*) He had no right to do that. There was no necessity for it. We would've helped him.

CHARLEY   (*grunting*) Hmmm.

BIFF   Come along, Mom.

LINDA   Why didn't anybody come?

CHARLEY   It was a very nice funeral.

LINDA   But where are all the people he knew? Maybe they blame him.

LINDA   Naa. It's a rough world, Linda. They wouldn't blame him.

LINDA   I can't understand it. At this time especially. First time in thirty-five years we were just about free and clear. He only needed a little salary. He was even finished with the dentist.

CHARLEY   No man only needs a little salary.

LINDA   I can't understand it.

BIFF   There were a lot of nice days. When he'd come home from a trip; or on Sundays, making the stoop; finishing the cellar; putting on the new porch; when he built the extra bathroom; and put up the garage. You know something, Charley, there's more of him in that front stoop than in all the sales he ever made.

CHARLEY   Yeah. He was a happy man with a batch of cement.

LINDA   He was so wonderful with his hands.

BIFF   He had the wrong dreams. All, all, wrong.

HAPPY   (*almost ready to fight* BIFF) Don't say that!

BIFF   He never knew who he was.

CHARLEY   (*stopping* HAPPY'S *movement and reply. To* BIFF) Nobody dast blame this man. You don't understand; Willy was a salesman. And for a salesman, there is no rock bottom to the life. He don't put a bolt to a nut, he don't tell you the law or give you medicine. He's a man way out there in the blue, riding on a smile and a shoeshine. And when they start not smiling back – that's an earthquake. And then you get yourself a couple of spots on your hat, and you're finished. Nobody dast blame this man. A salesman is got to dream, boy. It comes with the territory.

BIFF   Charley, the man didn't know who he was.

HAPPY   (*infuriated*) Don't say that!

BIFF   Why don't you come with me, Happy?

HAPPY   I'm not licked that easily. I'm staying right in this city, and I'm gonna beat this racket! (*He looks at* BIFF, *his chin set.*) The Loman Brothers!

BIFF   I know who I am, kid.

HAPPY   All right, boy. I'm gonna show you and everybody else that Willy Loman did not die in vain. He had a good dream. It's the only dream you can have – to come out number-one man. He fought it out here, and this is where I'm gonna win it for him.

BIFF   (*with a hopeless glance at* HAPPY, *bends toward his mother*) Let's go, Mom.

LINDA   I'll be with you in a minute. Go on, Charley. (*He hesitates.*) I want to, just for a minute. I never had a chance to say good-bye.

CHARLEY *moves away, followed by* HAPPY. BIFF *remains a slight distance up and left of* LINDA. *She sits there, summoning herself. The flute begins, not far away, playing behind her speech.*

LINDA   Forgive me, dear. I can't cry. I don't know what it is, but I can't cry. I don't understand it. Why did you ever do that? Help me, Willy, I can't cry. It seems to me that you're just on another trip. I keep expecting you. Willy, dear, I can't cry. Why did you do it? I search and search and I search, and I can't understand it, Willy. I made the last payment on the house today. Today, dear. And there'll be nobody home. (*A sob rises in her throat.*) We're free and clear. (*Sobbing more fully, released.*) We're free. (BIFF *comes slowly toward her.*) We're free ... We're free ...

BIFF *lifts her to her feet and moves out up right with her in his arms.* LINDA *sobs quietly.* BERNARD *and* CHARLEY *come together and follow them, followed by* HAPPY. *Only the music of the flute is left on the darkening stage as over the house the hard towers of the apartment buildings rise into sharp focus.*

CURTAIN

QUESTIONS AND EXPLORATIONS

1 Keeping Track

The questions in this section are designed to help your
reading and understanding of the play in the areas of plot,
character and interaction. They may be used as you read
the play or afterwards, for discussion or for writing. Some
are developed and expanded in the *Explorations* section.

Act One

1 How is Willy's condition described as he comes on
   stage?

2 How does Linda try to reassure him?

3 How does Willy explain his state of mind?

4 What does Linda suggest as a solution to the problem?

5 Why is Willy unwilling to accept this?

6 What is Willy's opinion of his own abilities?

7 Why had Willy and Biff argued earlier?

8 What is Willy's opinion of Biff?

9 What do Happy and Biff do for a living?

10 What is Happy's attitude to women?

11 What do we learn of Willy's relationship with Happy
   and Biff in their early years?

12 Who is the Woman?

13 Willy seems unsure of himself. Why?

14 How is Bernard contrasted with Biff and Happy?

15 Why does Charley come round to see Willy?

16 What are our first impressions of Ben?

17 Why does Linda accuse Biff of behaving badly towards Willy?

18 What did Linda find in the cellar?

19 Why does Biff agree to see Bill Oliver?

20 What is Willy's reaction to this?

Act Two

1 Why is Willy in financial difficulty?

2 Where is he meeting Biff and Happy?

3 What was the result of Willy's meeting with Howard?

4 What had Ben offered Willy and why did he reject it?

5 Bernard is again contrasted with Biff. What is the effect of this?

6 What happened when Biff went to meet Bill Oliver?

7 How does Willy behave when Biff recounts these events to him?

8 Why did the adolescent Biff visit his father in Boston?

9 Why did this visit change his opinion of Willy?

10 What happens in the restaurant?

11 Why is Willy planting seeds?

12 What is the only thing which Willy feels he had left to give Biff?

13 Why does Biff tell Linda and Willy he is leaving?

14 What are their reactions to this?

15 Why does Ben reappear at the end of this act?

16 Why does Biff cry?

17 How does Willy interpret his tears?

Requiem

1 How does Happy intend to continue his life?

2 Why is he 'deeply angered' as the stage directions for his first speech indicate?

3 Why does Charley say no one should blame Willy for his actions?

4 Linda's closing words are 'we're free'. What does she mean by this?

2 Explorations

The questions in this section are more detailed and rely upon your having read the whole play. Some of the questions develop ideas from the *Keeping Track* section. Because they tend to be more detailed, they offer the opportunity to develop the ideas into written, oral or practical coursework assignments. Some will require a close knowledge of the play; others will require a more imaginative response.

A Characters

Willy Loman

1 Identify the things which Willy considers to be important in life. Make a list of these and state where each one is revealed in the play.

2 What is your impression of the relationship between Willy and Biff? How had this relationship changed and why?

3 In Act Two, Biff calls Willy a 'phoney little fake'. How far would you agree or disagree with this statement?

4 Willy returns to the past on several occasions. Look at each of these 'visits' and say what they tell the reader about Willy.

5 In the Requiem, Biff says of Willy, 'He never really knew who he was'. What did Willy think he was? Was he correct in thinking this? Give clear reasons for your answers, referring closely to the play.

Biff Loman

1 Why does Biff agree to go and see Bill Oliver? What realisation does he come to about himself?

2 Biff changes in the course of the play. Begin with his schooldays and say exactly what these changes are. Give reasons for them if you can.

3 What is Biff's relationship with Linda? How does it affect the course of events in the play?

4 Biff has rejected the city for a simpler life in the country. Explain carefully why he has done this.

5 Willy describes Biff as a 'lazy bum' (Act One) who is 'spiting him' (Act Two). How far would you agree with this statement? Write two letters, one from Willy to Biff, setting out his accusations and one from Biff to Willy defending himself against them.

Happy Loman

1 Identify the things which Happy finds it impossible to do without. Why do you think he needs these things?

2 Happy says at Willy's graveside: 'It's the only dream you can have – to come out number-one man. He fought it out here, and this is where I'm gonna win it for him.' Discuss how likely you think this is.

3 Why does Happy still pin his hopes for success on Biff? Is he wise to do this?

4 Why do you think Happy learned nothing from Willy's death? What might he have learned which would have improved his life?

5 You are the manager of the firm which Happy works for. He has asked you for a reference to use in a job application. Write this reference, being as honest as you can, but being careful to support all you say with evidence from the play.

Linda Loman

1 Gather together all the evidence you can find about Linda's feelings for Willy. Write a short play script in which Linda defends him to a friend who is trying to point out his weaknesses.

2 At the very beginning of the play, Miller describes Linda as sharing Willy's longings. Try to pinpoint which of his dreams she shares, referring to the play to show where they occur.

3 Linda believes strongly that people should treat each other properly. Where does she make this clearest? Who is she accusing at the time and why?

4 Linda's speech at the end of the play shows that she has often failed to understand what has happened to Willy. Consider where and why this happens in the play.

5 Using the information you have gathered about Linda, try to imagine her in five years' time. What do you think she will be doing? Where might she be living? Will her ideas and ideals have changed at all? Write several diary entries for Linda, in which these questions – and any others you consider are important – are answered.

Ben Loman

1 Why do you think Ben has done so well in business, when Willy has not?

2 Ben seems to Willy a symbol of great success. Do you agree? (Consider here the sort of success Ben has had and how he has achieved it.)

3 Why does Ben appear in the play when he does? Make a chart, listing his appearances on one side and why you think Miller introduced him into the play on the other.

4 Show how the other characters react to Ben and explain their reactions. Miller made Ben invisible to many of the characters – why did he do this?

5 In what ways does Ben typify the Great American Dream?

Bernard

1 Who is Bernard compared unfavourably with at the beginning of the play?

2 What values does Bernard represent?

3 Why does he become successful?

4 Bernard was unable to help the Loman family at the beginning of the play – he is still unable to help them at the end! Give your opinions of this statement, supporting them with evidence from the play.

5 What is your opinion of Bernard? Give reasons for your answer.

Charley

1 Who is Charley contrasted with in the play?

2 What kind of solution does Charley offer to Willy? What solution would he really like to be able to give?

Howard Wagner

1 Why do you think Howard is so successful? Do you admire him for this, or not?

2 Why does Miller make the tape recorder an important item in the meeting between Howard and Willy?

3 Record a message from Willy to Howard contrasting his management style with that of his father.

The Woman

1 Why does the Woman have no name?

2 What is she most concerned about in the play?

3 Write a letter from the Woman to an agony aunt explaining her affair with Willy and her feelings for him.

4 How does her presence influence the course of events in the play? Is she an important character, or not?

B Themes

America as the land of opportunity and freedom

1 Willy has always believed America to be a country where anyone with ambition and energy can succeed. Despite this, he fails in what he has set out to do. Describe his ambitions and say why he is unsuccessful.

2 In America, all men may choose how they live: this is a type of freedom. What choices have Biff, Happy, Ben and Bernard made? Which does Miller want us to admire – and why?

3 Willy and Biff both dream about a good life in the country. Collect all the positive evidence about rural life and all the negative evidence about urban living. Discuss Miller's viewpoints in the play and decide his feelings about this issue.

Wealth

1 When Howard shows Willy his new tape recorder, Willy says 'I'm definitely going to get one' (Act Two.) Yet it is clear he cannot afford it. Show how Willy maintains the facade that all is well financially and explain why he feels obliged to do this.

Truth and lies

1 Willy hides behind his visions of the world and fails to realise the truth about himself and his family. How does he achieve this?

2 City life is seen by Miller as artificial and damaging. What is Biff's alternative to this way of life and why does he consider it to be superior?

3 Biff is destroyed by Willy's illusions. Explain how this happens.

C Criticism

1 Arthur Miller felt that the middle-class society which Willy lived in placed unreasonable demands on people, who felt that they had to conform to the idea of being successful. This meant making money with which to buy luxury goods and being looked up to by other members of society. Willy would have liked this sort of success but he could not achieve it.

Miller criticises society through Willy and suggests that change is needed if people are to feel valued and lead better lives. It has been said that the play provides no answers to this problem of change. How far would you agree that this is true? Be sure to give evidence for your opinions.

2 In *Death of a Salesman*, Miller tried to make us think again about the idea of tragedy. Tragic heroes in

Shakespeare's work have always been people of high birth with a fatal character flaw which caused them suffering and resulted in their deaths. Miller wanted his tragic hero – Willy – to be an ordinary man who tries to improve his lot and who gives up his life for what he believes.

Critics argue that this concept of tragedy is not as convincing as the more traditional model. Write what you feel about these opposing views, giving evidence from the play to support your answer.

3 We can see that Miller offers a new perspective on the idea of the tragic hero as Shakespeare saw it. Shakespeare's heroes left their audiences with lessons to be learned and the other characters in the plays gained knowledge and understanding. Critics accuse Miller of failing to do this in *Death of a Salesman*. Give your opinion referring closely to the play for your evidence.

OTHER TITLES IN THIS SERIES

Joyriders and Did You Hear the One About the Irishman? Age 14+

Christina Reid

'Mighty Belfast' is the setting for these two plays by Belfast-born playwright, Christina Reid. *Joyriders* is a hard-hitting play about four teenagers from the Divis flats in West Belfast, working on a youth scheme. Through jaunty, tense and often very funny dialogue the teenagers reveal their aspirations and dreams. In *Did You Hear the One about the Irishman?* Alison and Brian's families are linked by marriage but deeply divided by religion. Alison and Brian are warned that their relationship is dangerous but choose to ignore the threat to their lives ...

This edition has notes and assignments to help in meeting the requirements of Key Stage 4.

ISBN: 435 23292 4

The Play of Kes

Age 14+

Barry Hines and Allan Stronach

A straightforward and moving dramatisation of Barry
Hines' novel **Kes** in which fifteen year-old Billy trains a
kestrel. The training of the young hawk inspires feelings
of admiration and affection, emotions which neither his
family nor school offer. This edition comes with new
notes and assignments for Key Stage 4.

ISBN: 435 23288 6

The Play of Flowers for Algernon

Age 14+

Bert Coules

A powerful dramatisation of Daniel Keyes' story. Charlie is a retarded adult who desperately wants to be able to read and write. He undergoes a brain operation which increases his intelligence. But at what cost?

The original short story is included in this edition for comparison work. The play comes complete with notes and assignments to help in meeting the requirements of Key Stage 4.

ISBN: 435 23293 2

The Play of Animal Farm Age 14+

Peter Hall

This dramatisation of George Orwell's **Animal Farm** is fresh, funny and immensely enjoyable while retaining all the savagery of the original novel. Notes and assignments help in meeting the requirements of Key Stage 4. This edition also comes with lyrics by Adrian Mitchell and music by Richard Peaslee.

ISBN: 435 23291 6

The Best Years Of Your Life & Lives Worth Living
Age 14+

Clive Jermain
Lawrence Evans
Jane Nash

Each of these plays offers frank, perceptive and sometimes humorous insights into the life of a disabled person.

In *The Best Years of Your Life* Robert has cancer of the spine. As a member of the local football team he finds it difficult to meet his friends while sitting in a wheelchair. Throughout the play, Robert, his father and his brother, work out how to come to terms with his condition.

In *Lives Worth Living* Julie and her mentally-handicapped brother, Mark, are visiting the beach. During one short afternoon we see the whole range of joys and problems being with Mark involves. Through the lively, amusing dialogue between Julie and Mark we see the strong, mutual affection between them.

ISBN: 0435 23294 0

A Taste of Honey

Age 14+

Shelagh Delaney

A new edition of this popular classic play about the complex, conflict ridden relationship between a teenage girl and her mother, and the fleeting moments of affection and escape she finds.

This edition provides notes and assignment suggestions for GCSE.

ISBN: 0435 23299 1

Journey's End   Age 14+

R C Sherriff

Stanhope is hailed by his men as one of the best Captains in
the army. But as he and his officers sit in their dugout
awaiting attack, the full horror and futility of trench warfare
unfolds. This new edition provides notes and assignments
for Key Stage 4.

ISBN: 435 23290 8

Whose Life is it Anyway? Age 14+

Brian Clark

Whose Life is it Anyway? is both a powerful stage-play and major feature film about the struggle of the central character for the right to die.

Completely and permanently paralysed by an accident and dependent on a life-support machine, Ken Harrison challenges the traditional duty of the medical profession to keep him alive at all costs.

ISBN: 435 23287 8